Turkish Angora

Turkish Angora Cat Own

Turkish Angora cats care, personality, grooming,
health and feeding all included.

by

Henry Hoverstone

Published by: IMB Publishing

Table of Contents

Table of Contents 3

Foreword 7

Acknowledgements 8

Chapter 1: Introduction 9

Chapter 2: The Turkish Angora 10

   1) What is the Turkish Angora? 10

   2) Types of the Turkish Angora 11

   3) What to know before you get one 12

   4) Habitat 13

   5) The History of the Turkish Angora 13

   6) Anatomy and Lifespan of the Turkish Angora 14

Chapter 3: Physical Characteristics of the Turkish Angora 16

   1) Head 16

   2) Coat 16

   3) Color 17

Chapter 4: Personality and Behavior 19

   1) Why is it better to have an indoor Cat? 22

   2) Your New Turkish Angora and Other Cats 25

   3) Attention Seeking Disorder in Cats 27

   4) Getting Along With Other Pets 30

   5) Getting Along With Children 31

Chapter 5: Preparations for the Turkish Angora 32

Table of Contents

1) Essential supplies for the cat.. 32

2) Non-essential items.. 34

3) What to look for in a reputable breeder?.................................... 35

4) How to choose the Turkish Angora 36

5) Older Turkish Angora versus kittens.. 38

6) Where to find the Turkish Angora 40

7) Insurance and permits... 41

8) Pros and Cons of owning a Turkish Angora................................ 42

Chapter 6: Basic Care of the Turkish Angora Cat................................45

1) Introducing your kitten to your home 45

2) Basic care and routine.. 49

3) Astuteness.. 51

4) The Most Charming Cat 53

Chapter 7: Synopsis of the Turkish Angora Cat Character 55

Chapter 8: When a Turkish Angora is Pregnant 58

1) Reaching Puberty 58

2) Finding the Right Mate 59

3) Important Tips and Guidelines.. 60

4) Is my Turkish Angora in Labor? 61

5) Preparing for Birth 61

6) Danger signs 62

7) Things you must not do during pregnancy................................ 63

Chapter 9: Training the Turkish Angora 64

1) Litter box training... 64

2) Leash training.. 66

3) Teaching the cat tricks.. 68

4) Training a cat to learn new tricks 70

Chapter 10: Grooming the Turkish Angora **76**

1) Benefits of Grooming a Turkish Angora cat 77

2) Equipment needed for grooming a cat............................... 79

3) Handling and Safety Pointers.. 79

4) Can a Tranquilizer Work? 81

5) Types of Grooming for Turkish Angora Cats..................... 82

6) How to Brush the Fur of your Turkish Angora 84

7) Trimming the Nails of the Turkish Angora cat.................. 85

8) Dental Care 87

9) Eye Care of the Turkish Angora cat 87

10) Ear Care of the Turkish Angora cat............................... 88

11) Bathing the Turkish Angora cat.................................... 88

Chapter 11: Feeding the Turkish Angora **90**

1) Nutrition.. 90

2) Water 91

3) Proteins 92

4) Fats.. 93

5) Carbohydrates 94

6) Vitamins 94

7) Minerals 95

8) A Word About Milk.. 95

9) Give your cat a low fat diet 95

10) Keep a check on the treats 96

11) Say no to crash diets 96

12) Keep the activity levels high.. 96

13) Foods you must never give your cat................................ 99

Table of Contents

Chapter 12: Traveling with your Turkish Angora........104

    1) Traveling in a car.. 104

    2) Traveling by train 105

    3) Traveling by air.. 106

Chapter 13: Caring for the Turkish Angora 107

    1) Signs and symptoms of illness............................ 107

    2) What Causes Stress in Turkish Angora Cats?........ 110

    3) How to Reduce Emotional Stress in Turkish Angoras 111

    4) Examining for specific illnesses 115

    5) Medical Disorders 117

    6) Spaying and Neutering....................................... 119

    7) Vaccinations 123

    8) After Vaccination, What's Next? 125

Chapter 14 : Finding a Good Vet 127

Chapter 15. The Cost of Owning a Turkish Angora.......133

    1) Initial Costs... 133

    2) Optional Expenses... 134

    3) Ongoing Costs 135

    4) Insurance... 135

Conclusion 137

Foreword

My experience with the Turkish Angora cat inspired me to write an informative book on what I go through every day. Of course, I do not just go to the vet and follow all the requirements, but I always do my research before doing anything.

I hope this book teaches you how to take good care of your cat – whatever breeds they are. I know, every single breed differs on behavior, characteristics, feeding, personality – but they all require the same amount of attention and care. We, as people, feel neglected at times as well. Cats are no different.

I am confident that through the information that this book can offer you, you will have better experience and solutions in whatever it is that you are going through with your Turkish Angora.

Acknowledgements

I never had the chance to deal with animals until my little sister brought home a stray cat. I didn't know at the time but found out afterwards that it was a Turkish Angora cat.

I was a little bit annoyed because of the non-stop "meows" since the cat was in our house.

My biggest thanks goes to my sister as it was her who introduced me to the world of animals. I was never a fan of cats, until one day, I just thought of them as adorable. I learned how to be patient and my sincerity paid off when, little by little, they were increasing in numbers.

Hereby, I am sharing some insights and thoughts about my experience with taking care of cats. I have become a true cat lover.

Chapter 1: Introduction

Do you own a Turkish Angora cat? Do you want to own one? What information do you need before embarking on this journey of owning a cat? Are you a cat owner but you're not sure if the breed you have is a genuine cat breed of Turkish Angora? All these questions and more about the Turkish Angora will be discussed in this book.

In summary, you should expect to gain more knowledge on the history as well as the care of the Turkish Angora. Feeding patterns are important but which foods are best to give your cat, is it fish or meat? What allergies are susceptible with this cat breed?

A Turkish Angora is royalty in many parts of the world. As a caregiver or potential caregiver, questions on routines and basic care will be answered. As you read this book you will not only gain knowledge but tips as well to use when training your cat and keeping him/her happy.

After reading this book you will not hesitate to find this new companion as your trusted pet. Read on and get to learn more about the pedigree Turkish Angora cat

Chapter 2: The Turkish Angora

1) What is the Turkish Angora?

The Turkish Angora is a semi longhaired cat believed to have originated from Turkey. They are long bodied and graceful with a fine, silky coat. The white Turkish Angora is the most popular breed, but it also comes in a variety of other colors and patterns. Its intelligent and witty personality make it the perfect pet for a family with children.

The Turkish Angora is not a large cat and averages between 5 and 9 pounds. An overweight Turkish Angora is in danger of obesity and is more prone to diabetes. Thus, exercise is a crucial part of their daily routine. Its eye color differs and can range from brown to yellow to blue.

The Turkish Angora may suffer from blindness and can be deaf on one side. Nevertheless, they remain the most playful of creatures. If left alone, the Turkish Angora can become mischievous so it's advisable to have another cat breed to play with.

The agile nature of the Turkish Angora makes it an active climber. It climbs to the top of shelves and drawers, so for this reason you are advised to keep all bare cable wires covered. Although the cat is graceful in nature, it's also a loyal companion. The Turkish Angora may never leave your side. It's playful, requiring you to have many toys to keep it busy (we will discuss this in detail). A household with children is also a preferred environment for the cat.

The Turkish Angora is generally a clean cat so it's important to keep it in a clean environment.

2) Types of the Turkish Angora

It is typical to ask whether the Turkish Angora comes with a certain number of breeds or if it is singular in type. The determination or classification of breeds is done in different models scientifically, and to the pet lover, this might not be a factor. However, the breeders of such a revered breed have had to consider simple methods that create diversity but still preserve the status of the Turkish Angora cats.

The most common type is the white kind. However, after years and years of research and breeding, there is a growing relevance on the colored type. This popularity has led to the introduction of not only patched, spotted, or lightly colored cats, but those with solid colors as well. The most common ones include red, cream, blue, and black.

Hybridization is also a common phenomenon, leading to the emergence of cute, strong, and all sorts of mixed-characteristic breeds. These can thereof take different colors such as chocolate, lavender, and so on.

What I am sure of is that everyone has his or her taste when it comes to the choice, whether in breed, color, or type. These characteristics only act to provide more options for the pet lovers, and to make the experience more appealing and personal. To create a sentimental bond with the Turkish Angora, you have to let it choose you as they say.

3) What to know before you get one

Ask yourself; does it suit your demands as a person? Does it also suit your way of life, or rather; does it accentuate your personality? Sometimes, it may be a present for your kids, and the decision may not entirely lie on you on which to pick. However, a little guidance does no harm at all, pointing out the crucial features to keep an eye out for.

First and foremost, understand the temperament of this particular cat. Is this the first cat you are looking to buy? If not, how well do you relate to them? For most pet keepers, there is a mutual understanding that has to exist for a smooth co-existence. Due to the sensitivity and intelligence that the Turkish Angora exhibits, it demands a better persona from its owner than just upkeep. It can easily integrate with people of all kinds, whether old or young.

In addition, you need to understand that this cat is an attention seeker. Sometimes, it may tend to be "annoying" because of how it relates around other pets for those with multiple pets at home. This has led to some viewing it as an alpha cat.

Another important concept to keep in mind is that this cat tends to be independent and some individuals who are out looking for a lap or cuddle pet are in for a disappointment. This feature is also evident when it comes to its association with other pets.

Check on the condition of the cat before you decide to adopt one into your family. For instance, you could check out the color of the eyes of the Turkish Angora, which provides a hint as to whether it is blind or not.

These are the most common and prevalent things about Turkish Angora cats that any admirer or would-be owner deserves to know. Exemplify your experience with these cats by being passionate about their care and handling.

4) Habitat

The originality may vary depending on the individual or the theory you come across. The origin is not a mystery, however, as it is in its name. The major talking point is the conditions in which this cat can live in, with considerable attention to its immediate effect.

For a complete and satisfactory setting, the Turkish Angora cat can easily adapt to an apartment or a typical home. It should however be noted that some provisions are imperative to make it feel at home and well attended. These include toys to play with; a scratching post, and an occasional play outdoors. This component is available in greater detail in subsequent chapters of this book.

5) The History of the Turkish Angora

The Turkish Angora originates from Ankara, formerly Angora, in Turkey. Its long hair is associated with Turkey's cold weather, insulating them from the harsh conditions. Back in the 18th century, this cat was adorned by royalty and kept like true treasures. It is mainly confused with the Persian cat, whose physical traits are similar. Because of its physical features, the Turkish Angora has been sought out from Britain to France.

During the 1900s, the Turkish Angora became a common feature for most programs involving hybridization in Persia. This almost led to the extinction of the agile cat genus. Being a national treasure, programs begun towards the conservation of this cat.

The Turkish Angora continuously adapted to its environment by mutating its long hair for protection against the harsh conditions. Its survival in the mountainous regions of turkey brings out its resilient nature and its intelligent aspects. All these traits were passed down to their offspring, who are believed to have spread to

Persia, North America and Western Asia. All these perspectives are a result of the rich history surrounding the Turkish Angora.

For many years, the Turkish Angora was a phenomenon in cat shows. This entailed showing off their beautiful fur while showcasing the basic tricks. At that time, the population of the Angora cat began to decline. Because of this situation, the Turkish government established a breeding program for this rare breed. The Turkish government established a partnership with the Ankara zoo where this breed may be preserved.

In the zoo, the cats are kept under strict supervision as kittens are sold to people who can provide a good home for the cat. Over the years, the Turkish Angora has undergone inbreeding with the local cat population, giving rise to other new breeds of cats. The Turkish Angora has been certified as a pedigree cat. There are a variety of colors, white being the most popular. Others are spotted, tabby and bicolor patterns. The tabby pattern includes mackerel, classic, spotted and ticked or agouti tabby.

6) Anatomy and Lifespan of the Turkish Angora

The Turkish Angora is a natural breed of cats. A cat has nine lives is a statement you hear everywhere but as for the Turkish Angora, its lifespan is not stipulated and can live a long, healthy life. It's important to keep the cat in a clean environment as this will encourage and even motivate the cat to continue being playful.

Some lines in the Turkish Angora breed may inherit the heart disease feline hypertrophic cardiomyopathy (HMC), a fatal progressive heart condition. Although the symptoms are subtle, the first visible symptom is often sudden death. Veterinary schools of medicine are working to find ways to test, treat, and cure the disease. Currently, there is no cure available but medication can slow the progression if diagnosed early.

Turkish Angora Ataxia is a condition that begins at four weeks of age with tremors and progresses rapidly to complete lack of voluntary muscular control. This condition is also undergoing extensive research on possible treatments to be adopted. Currently there is no cure or treatment available.

Incompatibility blood types are common with Turkish Angoras as they posses both blood types A and B. This can be alarming, especially in times of breeding where kittens born under such conditions end up dying a few hours after the initial birth. The type B blood is also rare in the cat population, making it hard in times of emergency blood transfusion.

Deafness is not uncommon in pure white, blue-eyed or odd-eyed Angoras; the Turkish Angora is more prone to this than other pure white cats. Odd-eyed Angoras with one blue eye and one amber or green eye can lose hearing in one ear on the same side as the blue eye. Angoras with this disability should always be kept inside the home for protection. Even though they are deaf, Angoras do not lose their charm and continue with their playful nature.

A healthy Turkish Angora can live for many years if it does not acquire complications. It is essential as a caregiver to the Turkish Angora to ensure that the cat undergoes proper medical checkups to alleviate any types of illness associated. It has a life expectancy of 15-20 years.

Chapter 3: Physical Characteristics of the Turkish Angora

The Turkish Angora is one of the most beautiful cat breeds and has lived for many centuries. Its distinct features from the shape of the head to the rest of its body are articulate. Its thick fur coat is fine and very silky. Here we will discuss some of the unique features associated with the Turkish Angora and how to differentiate it from other cats.

1) Head

The Turkish Angora's head is small to medium sized, in balance with the length of its body. Its head shape is medium-long with a smooth wedge.

It has large, almond shaped eyes slanting upwards with an open expression. The eye color can be any shade of green, gold, green-gold, copper, blue or odd-eyed. The W gene responsible for the white coat and blue eye are closely related to its hearing ability. The presence of the blue eye can indicate the cat is deaf on that side although many of the blue and odd eyed whites have normal hearing. Deaf cats lead a normal indoor life.

Its ears are large, wide at the base and pointed. They are set closely together, high and erect, vertical on the head. It has a medium length nose with a chin gently rounded to form a perpendicular line with the nose.

2) Coat

A cat's fur is its crowning glory and a source of insulation. In the wild, a cat's coat color serves as camouflage and is related to its natural habitat. Chance color mutations and selective breeding have produced the variety of coats seen in today's pedigree cats.

Types of coat like the color is also developed to suit the habitat; the more rugged the climate, the thicker the coat.

The coat of the Turkish Angora is single coated. It is fine and silky that shimmers when the cat moves. Most Angoras are mainly white in color but other colors resulting from hybridization include lilac, chocolate and the pointed pattern with a combination of white. The Turkish Angora's coat is guarded and very long but finer and less profuse than the Persian.

The coat of the Turkish Angora is a single coat, which makes it easy to groom. The length of its coat is dictated by season. During hot weather, the Angora takes more of a short, hairy appearance. In the cold season, the coat grows longer and thicker as the britches and mane fluff up fully. Although the Turkish Angora is a longhaired cat, it does not mat easily since it's a single coat as opposed to double-coated cats.

3) Color

The Turkish Angora has one of more than twenty colors including black, blue and reddish fur. They come in tabby and tabby white along with smoke varieties and are in every other color other than those indicative of hybridization. Although, the Angora breed is known for its predominant white color.

There are two white genes; the dominant white and white spotting. These two genes are separated alleles that can occur in

17

the same cat. Hence a pure white cat can also be a spotted white cat. If the spotting gene occurs in the temple area of the cat's head, that ear will be deaf regardless of the eye color. This is true of non-dominant white cats, nevertheless in a dominant white cat there is no way to tell if the head is spotting gene white or dominant white.

You can only know this if breeding occurs and the kittens show the spotting gene. At least this information will help you eliminate the myth about associating white cats with blue eyes or odd-eyed as deaf.

Chapter 4: Personality and Behavior

The Turkish Angora's personality is as striking as its appearance, surpassing many other breeds when it comes to playfulness and affection. The Turkish Angora is an intelligent, adorable and very curious breed and is active throughout their life span. It may look slender and delicate but its solid muscular body stays fit by exercising its hunting instinct running around the house hunting a toy. Its extremely agile body makes it easy for the cat to climb and be found in unexpected high places. It's important to be attentive to the Angora cat, as they love attention.

A Turkish Angora keeps his kitten-like playfulness well until his old age. It is friendly towards guests, it is a sociable breed best suited to home with another cat. A bored Turkish Angora can cause a lot of mischief, thus it's important not to leave the cat alone for many hours. It's affectionate and always ready to help and participate in all your activities. When it wants to play, the Turkish Angora can be very persistent and can be destructive just to get the desired attention.

Their intelligence enables them to devise ways of opening doors, cabinets and drawers. They have a tendency of concealing themselves in surprising places including closets or even in the cloth basket, which for them is play. A happy Turkish Angora rolls over on its back with its feet kneading joyfully in the air, accompanied with an extremely loud purr.

A fair fact about the Angora is even though it is a social cat, it is not a lap cat. This simply means that it does not like to be held for more than a few minutes. It does, however, prefer staying close or remaining in the room with you. In short, the Turkish Angora loves to snuggle. Cats cannot talk but the Turkish Angora is one breed that loves to talk. It can be very vocal and can carry out an animated conversation for the longest time. Described as a ballerina, the Angora cat loves to dance and responds positively to music. It walks in coordinated grace of a ballet dancer in furry shoes.

Turkish Angora cats are indoor cats by choice. It actually loves being indoors, cuddled up in the warmest corners of your home. Unlike most cats, the Turkish Angora is not an independent cat. It does not like being left in the open for too long.

Even if you do take your Turkish Angora out occasionally, you must make sure that you are around it all the time, as these cats tend to feel a sense of despair when they are alone. The best way to take a Turkish Angora out is with the leash on. Although this may seem unusual for a cat, it is a common practice among Turkish Angora owners.

There are several reasons why people think that keeping a cat indoors is unfair. Some of the most common myths associated with keeping a cat indoors are:

A lack of exercise can lead to weight issues. – It is not mandatory for a cat to go outdoors to get the exercise that it requires. Especially with a breed like the Turkish Angora; it is very easy to prompt them to stay active even indoors. All you need to do is place a cat tree that he/she can climb. Cats also love to sharpen their claws on these cat trees. Turkish Angora cats are naturally playful.

This means that you can give them toy mice and other pet toys to play with. Even a spool of thread or a paper box can become a great play tool for your pet. The most important thing with an indoor cat is the environment that it lives in. If you can make your home comfortable for the cat to run around and play in, you need not worry about taking him/her outdoors for some exercise.

It is not possible to domesticate a cat to stay indoors. – This is not true, especially with the Turkish Angora Cat. This breed opts to stay indoors. As for the sunshine and natural environment required by them, they will just enjoy these sights and sounds

20

from a windowsill. One of the most important Turkish Angora cat characteristics is that it can be walked with a harness.

So, you don't even have to worry about getting the cat the amount of outdoor time that it requires. Most cat breeders might recommend an enclosure to keep your cat safe outdoors. However, with a Turkish Angora there is absolutely no need to use any cage or enclosure.

The pet might urinate and dirty the house up. – Cats, as a species, are very easy to toilet train. All you need to do is teach them to use the litter box. With an intelligent cat like the Turkish Angora, there is no need to worry about getting the cat toilet trained. One thing that most cat owners observe is that after sometime, the cat urinates outside the box.

This is only an indication that the litter box is too dirty. It is the cat's way of telling its owner that it is time to have the litter box cleaned up. Most owners think that this behavior is an indication that the cat needs to go outside. Sometimes, it could be an indication that your cat may have some medical requirements. If your cat continues to litter outside the box even after you have cleaned it, make sure you consult a veterinarian.

The cat might scratch and ruin the furniture. – It is true that cats love to keep their claws sharp. So, it is natural for them to scratch hard surfaces as a mechanism to trim and sharpen their claws. If your cat is not trained, then you can expect your furniture to be ruined in just a few days. The solution to this does not come from trimming the nails of your cat. The behavior will persist. The best thing to do would be to provide your cat with a cat tree. In case your cat continues to damage other surfaces in spite of providing it with a tree, you must observe the types of surfaces that he/she likes to sharpen his/her nails on.

All you need to do is cover the cat tree with that material. Each cat has its own preference when it comes to the material that it chooses to scratch. In order to train your cat to use only the cat tree, you may also spray scents like catnip in order to attract the cat to the tree.

It is unhygienic to have a cat at home. – Cats usually tend to walk on high surfaces like kitchen cabinets and shelves. In case you do not find this comfortable or hygienic, you can train the cat to only occupy certain spaces. It is also possible to train your cat to stay away from the kitchen.

In any case, cats are extremely clean creatures. They are constantly bathing or cleaning themselves. Another thing with an indoor cat, Turkish Angora, for example, is that the amount of contaminants that it brings in is a lot less than an outdoor cat.

Cats infect pregnant women. – One very common reason for most people to keep cats outdoors is the presence of a pregnant woman in the household. Many believe that women who are pregnant can contract a disease called Toxoplasmosis if they come into contact with cat feces by accident.

Unknown to many, this disease is most often caused by the consumption of uncooked meat. However, in order to be safe, pregnant women should always wear gloves while cleaning litter boxes. The cat is not a threat to the well-being of the pregnant woman and can be allowed to stay indoors without the danger of any infection.

Now that we have busted the myths about indoor cats, you might also want to consider some rather logical reasons to keep your cat indoors. When you have a cat like the Turkish Angora that loves to stay indoors, you will never have to really worry about the well being of your cat.

1) Why is it better to have an indoor Cat?

There are several reasons why an indoor cat like the Turkish Angora is a more convenient option. Here are a few things that you might want to consider if you are thinking of choosing an outdoor cat over an indoor cat:

Traffic is one of the biggest reasons to keep a cat indoors. – If you live close to a highway or reside on a street that is relatively busy, you might want to consider a Turkish Angora that will spend most of its time indoors. Even the smallest accident can be fatal for your cat or might result in serious injuries.

Cats that roam outdoors are most susceptible to infections from other cats. – Feline Immunodeficiency Virus or Feline Leukemia is quite common in cats that roam outside. These diseases are usually transmitted from one cat to another. Both the diseases mentioned above are fatal for cats. If you allow your cat to roam freely, there are also several possibilities of catfights with other stray cats in the neighborhood.

This leads to injuries and abscesses that make it hard for both the owner and the Turkish Angora. Not only do these injuries cause a lot of pain to your pet, they will also cost you several hundreds of dollars to take care of and treat. If your cat has not been properly vaccinated, then it runs the risk of several other diseases that are prevalent in the outdoors.

Parasites are common issues faced by cats. It is very easy for fleas to attack your cat if it is usually strolling freely outdoors. – Some fleas may also carry diseases that are deadly for the cat as well as its owners.

Some ticks also have the potential to paralyze the cat permanently or even kill it if not treated correctly. Fungi like ringworm can also infect your cat. Ringworm can be passed on from the cat to its owner quite easily. Although it is not a deadly disease, ringworm usually recurs in cats and is not easy to treat or get rid of.

If your cat is outdoors often then there are several other dangers that it will encounter. – Domesticated cats are usually not able to defend themselves against animals like dogs, opossums and snakes and will either end up being seriously injured or even die due to these attacks. If your cat ventures into wrong territories by mistake, it becomes vulnerable to these attacks. Cats are also susceptible to attacks from people as well.

A cat that is allowed to roam outdoors is more likely to get lost. – They may also be stolen to be used in labs. In many horrifying instances, cats are killed for trade of fur and even extremist religious practices. So it is best that you either opt for a cat that stays indoors or at least ensure that it has a collar with information to identify it. According to statistics, close to 10% of cats rescued in animal shelters are not reclaimed by their owners.

Skin cancer is also a problem with most cats that go outdoors. – In the case of cats with dark fur, the threat of skin cancer due to excessive exposure to the sun is more prevalent. If you live in a country or a part of the world where skin cancer is highly prevalent, you must consider protecting your cat from exposure to sunlight. Many cat owners neglect the importance of keeping a cat in an enclosure when left outdoors. You must ensure that the enclosure has enough space for the cat to rest in the shade.

You might also face several social problems when you allow your cat to roam outside. – It is possible that your cat litters your neighbor's garden or simply ruins a beautiful flowerbed. In either case, you might find yourself quarrelling endlessly with your neighbor. It is impossible to locate and control a cat that is used to the outdoors.

Although there are several myths surrounding the need for cats to be aloof and independent in the outdoors, you can prove them all wrong with your Turkish Angora cat. The fact that the cat loves to stay with its owners shows that it is made to be indoors.

If you feel like your cat is getting bored of the indoors, all you have to do is put in a bit of effort to make the environment more interesting. Especially with a highly intelligent cat like the Turkish Angora, you must try to include puzzle toys and other stimulating activities in its routine. You must make sure you spend time with your Turkish Angora to keep him/her healthy and happy.

2) Your New Turkish Angora and Other Cats

If there is already a resident cat in your home, expect the Turkish Angora to become more dominant with familiarity. It is stressful to your old pet to deal with the fact that there is another cat in the house. Quite obviously, it is stressful for you as well to make sure that your pet does not feel neglected or out of place. You need to take each step at a time to make the situation more relaxed for you, your older cat and the your new Turkish Angora.

The first direct interaction should be scheduled over a weekend. – This will make sure that you have all day to spend with the new cat and your resident cat. You can make sure that there are no unpleasant interactions. It is always best to have these interactions during mealtimes. You can expect some growling and hissing but it will not be entirely aggressive. To make sure that it does not get out of hand, you must place the feeding bowls at opposite ends of the room. Once the feeding is done, separate them instantly.

Cats are territorial by nature. So make sure you establish the boundaries for both cats. – When your new cat is out of the confinement from its bonding room, you might want to make a special corner for him that is not too close to the existing space of you resident cat. Just place the feeding bowl and the cat bed in the designated area with your cat's favorite toys.

The interactions between your cats must be gradual. –You can try the blanket switching technique with cats as well. When they are accustomed to each other's scent, they become comfortable with each other. You must allow them to spend more time with each other slowly. Only when you are assured that they are relaxed in each other's company, you can leave them unsupervised. Until then, you must never leave them unattended in the same space. This is especially true for night times.

If you have more than one cat at home, you will notice that one of the resident cats will take the initiative to introduce the new cat to the existing group.

It is common for the cats to not get along immediately. If this is true for your resident cats and the new kitten, make sure you do not punish either of them. Just separate them when they get anxious. You must understand that this behavior is purely instinctive. With regular interactions, the cats will learn to live together peacefully.

When you see cats fighting amongst themselves, you will not consider it a big deal. This is especially true when you own more than one cat. However, it is wise to be watchful when your pets get into a fight.

You have to ensure that the fight does not turn ugly. This, much like a human brawl, can have serious repercussions. Catfights are mostly attributed to fear, territorial understanding, stress venting, anxiety display etc. There are various kinds of aggression that are seen in cats.

Sexual aggression – Sexual aggression in animals is quiet a common phenomenon. However, in cats it is not very commonly seen. However, when two cats get sexually aggressive towards each other, the dominating cat bites the victim cat's nape and there is an attempt to climb on the victim cat.

Territorial aggression – This sort of aggression is also observed quiet often amongst all animals. Much like dolphins, dogs etc. cats are also known to mark their territory. Cats urinate to mark their territory. The dominating cat is seen hissing, growling and readying himself to jump on his victim.

Usually, the trespassing cat turns around respectfully and walks away. In some cases, the victim or the trespasser cat will put up a fight and things turn ugly. One interesting thing to note is: the cat that marks its territory need not be the oldest cat or the cat that has lived in the house for the longest period of time.

3) Attention Seeking Disorder in Cats

Cats are known to 'meow' nonstop at certain times of the day or night. Their constant howling can become a nuisance for the owner. Before one jumps the gun, and comes to the worst conclusion, it is sensible to sit down and understand what is causing your cat to behave in this particular manner.

The howling of your cat can be broadly categorized as either crying or meowing. The cause for such behavior can be either emotional or physical pain that the cat is experiencing. Experts have noted that the attention-seeking demeanor of the cats can be further classified as follows.

Mournful howl – Some cats tend to howl in the night like they are calling out for help. This particular howl can make the cat owner cringe with sympathy for the poor creature. This mournful howl is mostly a result of deafness. In some cases, this cry has been identified as the cat's cry for help in its old age. It is also associated with the insanity of an old cat. The reason for this howl need not always be an emotional one.

A certain condition called as Feline hyperesthesia is also associated with this behavior. When a cat howls during the night and is found to roll around in the house, you must consider this condition. This condition is commonly called Rippling Skin Disorder. This disorder is considered a stress disorder. However, the symptoms usually include a set of unrelated issues. The cats tend to become extremely sensitive to touch and the skin begins to show ripples.

The possible causes of this disorder are the excessive presence of unsaturated fatty acids in combination with Vitamin E deficiency, brain infection or trauma, and flea allergies. If the cat is diagnosed with this disorder then it is unlikely that it will be completely cured. So, paying attention to these issues can help you provide greater comfort to the cat and keep tab on its behavioral issue.

Chronic pseudo hunger – Hunger pangs are commonly observed in cats as well. Like human beings, cats also have food cravings, which are unwarranted. Cats tend to develop a lot of liking towards some treats, such as tuna flakes. This can also turn into an addiction of sorts.

The figure 8 – Cats are known to run around their owner's feet in circles. This is also categorized under attention seeking issues of the cat. They are much like kids who need a little bit of extra attention. They also tend to rub themselves against your arm when they need extra attention.

Meow chat – Cats are very vocal. They also like to have conversations with their owners. Some chatty cats tend to prod their owners into lengthy conversations. If the owner refuses to spend enough time with the cat, then it tends to suffer from excessive loneliness.

Scratching – Cats scratch. This is common knowledge. Sometimes they overdo it and then the owner may have to be a little concerned. Excessive scratching can cause the cats to bleed from their skin. It has been noted that cats use scratching as a tool to demand for your attention. It is best to take note of this behavior before your beloved pet inflicts physical pain on itself.

Contrary to traditional belief, a cat that stays indoors is known to be healthier and happier. Considering all the threats that you are protecting it from, there is no reason why you should not believe this. Research proves that cats that are allowed to stay indoors also have a longer life than cats that are allowed to roam freely.

However, there are some cat owners who are not particularly fond of keeping the cat indoors. Turkish Angora cat owners, however, must be willing to keep them in the house. If you are insistent on having a Turkish Angora cat but are uncertain about keeping it indoors, you must ensure that you provide it with a good enclosure.

This is the only way to ensure that your cat gets the benefits of staying outdoors while being protected from the dangers that are prevalent. We will discuss in detail about cat enclosures in the following Chapters.

The Turkish Angora is the best pet because of its loyalty, devotion and affection. It makes a good companion even in times when you're sick. It will be there to nurse you back to health. Its amazing personality is what makes its owners spend more time with it. They are affectionate to their owners and can relate well to other humans as well but the full adoration falls on the owner.

If you love to stay home, you must definitely opt for a Turkish Angora cat. This beauty is extremely active and social. They will actually put in sincere efforts to seek your attentions. As a result, Turkish Angora cats have the tendency to develop idiosyncrasies that are extremely adorable and quite entertaining.

For instance, if your Turkish Angora notices that you find it funny when he/she chases a spool of thread, you can expect him to do it over and over again. They will also condition their behavior to appeal to the entire family. As long as he has your attention, you can be sure that your Turkish Angora will entertain you quite gladly.

A Turkish Angora cat is also quite adept at finding ways to keep itself entertained when it gets bored. This medium sized kitty is packed with energy and requires constant stimulation to expend that energy.

What happens if you simply get bored of its antics? Well, he/she will just voice out his/her dissatisfaction at your lack of attention. Turkish Angora cats are highly vocal cats. They are not, in the slightest bit, noisy or annoying. They are just highly responsive by nature. Their call is not the regular "meow" that you expect from a cat.

The call of a Turkish Angora cat is rather shrill and unique. The intensity of their purring and calling will also change with their mood. For instance, if you have just come back from work, your Turkish Angora will smother you with affection, purring loudly and following you around the house.

With a Turkish Angora cat, you will find yourself a true companion. They are very patient creatures that are extremely attached to their owners. They like to be played with, cared for and loved. The most amazing thing about the Turkish Angora is that it is a highly understanding cat that is sensitive enough to react to your moods perfectly. If you are happy, your Turkish Angora will rejoice with you. If you are upset, your Turkish Angora will curl up close to you and will never leave your side. Overall, this is one of the most compassionate cat breeds that you can ask for.

This amazing cat breed has the most entertaining personality in comparison to other breeds. It may also be a challenge to have this cat as a pet due to its short attention span. The Turkish Angora desires interaction and play. It loves to swim in the wild and is well known for pouncing on fish in rivers. Even at home, they seem to enjoy the bathtub when they are taking a bath.

4) Getting Along With Other Pets

The Turkish Angora is known for being a cat that is able to get along with other animals. It can do fine with many pets and will not pick fights if the pet is relaxed and introduced to these other pets. However, it is important to ensure that the cat is not going to be too irritated around other pets. It is often easy for a Turkish Angora to want to exhibit its dominance. That is, it wants to be the main focus of attention in just about any space that it is in. It's a peculiar point that is interesting for all to explore and think about.

5) Getting Along With Children

Turkish Angoras will also get along with children quite well. They are relaxed and will enjoy being with them throughout the day.

However, children who are more active will be better suited to such a cat. The Turkish Angora is known to be relatively active and will not want to relax on one's lap for too much time. In fact, some cats might not listen to children as they tell them to do certain things. It's an interesting aspect that shows just how such a cat can behave.

Chapter 5: Preparations for the Turkish Angora

Preparing to bring a new member of the family home can be a whirlwind of an experience if you don't have the required information. Here I will list some of the essential and non-essential supplies you may need. A Turkish Angora is a very playful cat and it needs lots of attention but as a human being, you may not have much time due to work and other schedules. When you make the decision to buy or adopt a Turkish Angora, below are some of the essential supplies you will need.

1) Essential supplies for the cat

Supplies for the cat can be divided into two parts; the essential and non-essential items required.

a. Scratching Post
A scratching post is important, especially for playful cats such as the Turkish Angora. It is classified as an essential item because it's an important playtime for the Turkish Angora. A scratching post will save you from torn furniture cushions associated with play with the cat.

b. Litter Box
A litter box is the most important item and each cat owner must have one. A litter box is the relieving point of a cat and it should be strategically located. In the next Chapters we will discuss the

different approaches to take when litter training your cat. Home breaking a cat can be cumbersome, especially when your rag smells of cat urine.

A well-trained cat does not urinate outside of its litter box. So, when this happens and you have determined that it is a behavioral problem, then you can take the following measures:

Check the litter box and clean it if you have left it without any plans for appropriate cleaning.

Do not make the cat smell its own urine as a punishment. This is nothing but bullying your pet and such behavior will serve no purpose.

Check if your cat is stressed. Any change in its environment causes stress in them. They react very promptly to new family members, renovation of the house etc.

If you find your cat taking a liking for a particular spot in the house, then place the litter box in that area.

Give your cat some more attention. This maybe its way of attracting your attention as it has been missing your company.

c. A Cat Carrier

A cat carrier is described as the cat transportation. It's an essential item because it will help you when transporting your new cat home from the pet shop. During trips, it's important that your cat is comfortable to avoid becoming a nuisance. Cat carriers come in different sizes so make sure you consult the pet shop owner to get more perspective on the carrier.

d. Brush and Fine Comb

Grooming your cat is an important part of bonding. A brush and fine toothcomb are essential, especially with double-coated cats that tend to mat. The Turkish Angora, however, due to its single coat is easy to groom and take care of. They may need to be brushed once or twice a week. The topic of grooming will be discussed in detail in the next Chapters.

e. Cat Pillow
Just as you need comfort on a place of rest, buying a cat pillow will be a great investment. This is mainly because a cat pillow will discourage the cat from laying everywhere in the house, leaving balls of hair. The Turkish Angora is a playful cat and it requires adequate comfort. It's also important to keep its sleeping environment very clean.

f. Food and Water Dishes
Cats associate a place they are given food as their home. It's essential to have cat dishes as they feel good when offered food. This will help build a relationship of trust that increases on bonding with your cat.

2) Non-essential items

a. Cat Collar
A collar acts as an identification document for a cat. A cat collar should include the cat owner's name, a reachable number and the cat's name. This way, if the cat ever strayed, the owner may be contacted to pick it up with no worries.

b. Shampoos
A Turkish Angora is not the most complicated animal to take care of. A wash for this cat breed can be between every eight to twelve weeks. Understanding the right kind of shampoo to use on these occasions is important. Harsh shampoos may affect the silky fur of the Turkish Angora cat.

c. Toys
The Turkish Angora is a playful cat and requires many toys. Recommendations include fake mice, which give them great hunting skills. Cats are social creatures and interacting by playing with toys is a great way to create a bond with the cat.

All these supplies are essential in one-way or the other. After buying all these essentials you can go ahead and buy the Turkish Angora cat and create a great environment. But before you do that, here are some pointers on what to look for when purchasing this animal.

3) What to look for in a reputable breeder?

An ideal breeder will follow the required code of ethics that stops him/her selling it to any pet store or to any wholesaler and he/she fulfills all his/her responsibilities. Whenever you want to buy a Turkish Angora, look for a breeder who has health certification to know if there is any genetic disease in any of the cats, loves being around them, and also who raises them in their own house rather than in some pet store or some storage room. This is important because of the fact that cats that are raised in an isolated place are fearful and they take more time to socialize with people.

When it comes to a good breeder, many of them have a website of their own, which makes it very difficult for a person who is trying to buy Turkish Angora to decide which one is good and which one is not.

You need to look into the breeder too. It's reputation as a cattery and the hygienic conditions of the facility. The bloodline would also be a factor that you would like to consider before buying your Angora.

Then of course, the color and pattern of the fur and the eye color would be something that you might like to have according to your likeness. These factors also affect the price of the cat. Normally, Angora cats range in price between two hundred to eight hundred dollars. For instance, the rare blue eyed and hearing Angora is considerably expensive to buy than other ones. The white deaf Angora however will not only be very easily available, but also cheaper to buy.

Be very careful when buying yourself a cat. Take all things into account. Do not in any case rush into buying. The major problem that you may come across is finding a reliable cattery. It is so difficult these days to distinguish between the unreliable and reliable breeders. There is nothing you can really do that can guarantee that you don't end up buying an unhealthy kitten, but by going about the things in the right way you can certainly reduce the chances.

Firstly, do a thorough research on what breed you want to buy, so that you know what is coming. Secondly, check out the facility very meticulously to see if there are any unhygienic conditions or sick animals in the house. Then you need to know what to ask the breeder. Asking the right questions can spare you a lot of trouble. Asking your veterinarian can also be a good idea. He can refer you to a reputable breeder that he might know himself.

As it has been mentioned earlier, do not show any haste. Be patient. The breed that you are looking for might take a while to be made available to you. The breeders often do not give away kittens unless they are at least twelve to sixteen weeks of age. Kittens can be fun but at the same time, they can be disaster too, until they become somewhat adult. So an adult Turkish Angora cat might be exactly what you need.

4) How to choose the Turkish Angora

It is very important that you know everything about the cat that you are going to buy so that you are sure about buying the right one.

While buying, many people confuse the Turkish Angora cat with the Persian cat even though there is quite a lot of difference between the two. Persian is a heavy and a peaceful cat while Angora is small, normally having a weight ranging from 4-10 pounds. The body of an Angora is long, eyes large, and ears are pointed.

The sizes of both these cats are also different, the Persian cat having a large head with a flat face and the Angora having a small head placed nicely on the neck. So do keep these things in mind and don't confuse the Angora with the Persian cat.

Turkish Angora cats are highly agile. They do not like to sit around much. They like heights. Often, they would be spotted perched high on some cupboard or something. They enjoy swimming too. They are known for their natural swimming ability. However, upbringing matters a lot.

Cats having swimming mothers often tend to learn swimming easier than others. These cats are very friendly. They build association with their owner very soon. One striking feature of Angora cats is their long hair. However, they aren't going to be a trouble. Their fur doesn't mat easily because of the absence of a downy undercoat. This can be one feature that can help you distinguish Angora from other long-haired cats.

When buying a Turkish Angora cat, do look for deafness because it is common in white, blue eyed Angora cats but this is not only for Turkish Angora cats – it is quite common in every type of white cat having blue eyes. This has been going for quite a long time in this type of Turkish Angora cat because of the defect in the dominant gene, which is responsible for their white color and blue eyes. This gene has linked itself to hereditary deafness of the cat through their organ of Corti in cochlea.

The cats with odd-eyes, like one blue and the other perhaps green, generally tend to lose their ability to hear in one ear, provided they inherit the defective gene. These cats, with defective hearing, however, adapt very easily since they very effectively use their senses of taste and smell. They also depend more on their body language than humans do. So hearing loss does not take away the communication power of a cat.

The fur of the Turkish Angora is fine and silky. The body of the Turkish Angora is longer than the Persian cat and more graceful. The head of the Angora is small and wedge shaped towards the chin. It has almond shaped eyes that come in different colors. Their tail is long and full of fur with the tip almost touching the head.

Be sure to look for the fur turfs on the ends of its ears. As you look at other breeds, these are some of the features that you can use to choose the true Turkish breed. In terms of color, due to permutation and mutations, the Turkish Angora can be found in other colors including brown, smoky or spotted. There is no difference but be sure to look out for the above features.

5) Older Turkish Angora versus kittens

Adult cats are very different from kittens. They will take longer to get used to the household and the people living there. Whether you have rescued or adopted an older cat, there are simple tips and tricks that will help you make the cat feel comfortable. Remember that an adult cat comes with several past experiences.

Its behavior will depend entirely on the kind of interactions that he/she has had with people in the past. You can do a little background check and make necessary adjustments in your lifestyle to accommodate an adult cat.

You should ask your breeder or the owner of the pet rescue centre all the details of your cat's history. – There may be specific toys that the cat is fond of. There may also be special scents or fragrances that the cat might require to feel comfortable. It is also important to know if your cat pet-to-be has had an abusive history. If yes, you must understand completely the things that might make the cat anxious or uncomfortable.

You can keep the adult cat in a cat carrier for a few days. – In case there is a specific bonding room for the new cat, make sure you leave the carrier there. This can become your cat's permanent hideout and also zone of comfort.

The litter box, food and water must be introduced to the new adult cat. – Place them all in the bonding room or confinement room of the cat.

When your cat is ready, you can take it to new parts of your home. – It is absolutely mandatory that you familiarize the cat with all areas of your home. For an indoor cat like the Turkish Angora, especially, being able to look for resting spots and hiding spots becomes possible only when he is comfortable with all the space available.

With an adult cat, conditioning becomes necessary. – The responsibility is on you to make sure that the cat spends ample time around you. You must make time to play with the cat, talk to him and just be around him. A Turkish Angora cat requires more attention that other cats and you must try as hard as you can to keep him happy. Only when the cat is sure of you as the right companion, it will open up and be friendly.

Make sure you keep an eye on your new cat. – If it does not eat properly or use the litter box, you might have to seek some help from an expert. Another common problem with adult cats is the development of skin problems. These are all signs of discomfort and unhappiness in the cat.

With a Turkish Angora cat, it is easier to overcome these special requirements. This is why it is considered the ideal pet for people who need constant companionship.

Older Turkish Angoras are more mature and understand easily when it comes to litter training and learning new tricks. The more mature Turkish Angora is able to understand the environment better and requires little attention.

Kittens require a lot of attention and care at this age while still adapting to the home environment. New environments easily frighten them and in the next Chapter we will discuss the introduction of the cat in the home. Adult cats can attack the new baby cat so it's important for the owner to introduce this new pet without making it look like a competition.

Kittens need a lot of warmth as they grow; therefore, you will need to buy a heater to keep the room warm for the Turkish Angora. The grooming of the adult and kitten Turkish Angora are the same; light brushing once or twice a week. Kittens are generally playful and will require tons of toys to keep them busy all the time. Adult Angoras are very social and interactive as well.

The choice between an adult and the kitten are dependent on time. If you have time, you can choose to buy a kitten and enjoy the journey, as a healthy Turkish Angora can live for 15 to 20 years. An adult Angora cat is not time consuming and maybe a good choice for busy couples and senior citizens who have no energy to train a cat.

6) Where to find the Turkish Angora

True breeds of the Turkish Angora originated from Turkey. Mutations and interbreeding by Britain and France brought into play the same pedigree of the Turkish Angora cat. Turkish Angoras are mainly found in breeding camps and some pet shops. They cost up to $800 dollars to buy a true breed of the Turkish Angora. So where can you find the Turkish Angora cat breed?

The cat fanciers association certifies breed clubs that breed pure cat pedigrees. Some well known breeders include the Catchannel.com. The website has lots of information on getting a cat, cat health, cat behavior all you need to know about cats is on this website.

The website also shares information on other states where you can easily call or go through the website for more information. Even though the Turkish Angora is a rare breed it's important to ensure breeders have the required certificates of the pedigree cat.

Pets4home is another site where you can easily find a pure bred Turkish Angora in the UK. You have the option to adopt or buy the on sale cats. Prices range between 100 to 300 pounds. The website emphasizes the need for certificates when it comes to purchasing the animal.

If you are planning on adopting the Turkish Angora, you can check out the following sites. Cat adoption team, pet smart and the pet finder have listed thousands of pets available for adoption. Adopting a cat is a big step for anyone so it's important to prepare well, that way you have all the required essentials for when the cat arrives home.

7) Insurance and permits

Pet insurance for purebred cats costs more than for mixed breed cats. Purebred cats are more likely to make claims for hereditary conditions that may be expensive to treat. One of the companies that provide pet insurance is Embrace pet insurance, where you can choose a plan that fits you. The plan can be annually maximum, deductible and reimbursement percentage.

Some of the benefits of pet insurance are that they are covered under breed-specific conditions, cancer treatment, diagnostic testing and imaging, surgery, hospitalization and nursing care, alternative therapies and ER & special care. It's important to do more research on the best pet insurance company to use in your country.

As you make the purchase, ask yourself if you can afford it if your cat is involved in an accident or ill. Costs of vet visits can range from $280 dollars with complex treatments costing over $3000 dollars. Some of the recommended insurance companies include Healthy pets, Argos pet insurance, Churchill insurance, Debenhams personal finance and pet protect. They offer a personalized coverage according to the needs of the cat.

Pedigree papers and the breeder's name important documents while purchasing the Turkish Angora. Papers are important

41

because some of the commercially bred kittens may develop disease or temperament problems. Some may suffer from physical defects or come up with hereditary weakness.

Some of the main things to check when insuring your cat include vet fees; pet insurance excess fees, lifetime cover, pet age limits and other additional benefits. Vet fees can be expensive if your pet needs treatment but with a pet insurance policy your vet fees are paid by the insurance policy.

Pet insurance policies include excess fees; it can be $50 or even more. If the visit costs you $150, you will first pay $50 while the insurance company will pay the other $100. It is better to look for policies that have lower excess fees that meet your needs.

Coverage for life policies are important so make sure you understand the benefits well. The lifetime cover insurance policy is often much more expensive than the standard cover for 12 months. A standard insurance policy covers only the first year, when your pet develops a long-term illness when the policy is renewed, the illness would be treated as an existing illness.

Few pet insurance companies have a maximum age limit for pets they will insure. Some companies may not offer coverage for pets with a maximum of 10 years. Additional benefits may include cattery fees, rewards cost when a pet goes missing or even offer money for advertising. Pet insurance is definitely something you should consider when buying a Turkish Angora.

8) Pros and Cons of owning a Turkish Angora

The Turkish Angora cat has become such a rare and hard to come by breed that it is now seen as a crime to take them out of their country of origin, Turkey. These cats are an ancient and natural breed of domestic cat. Their lineage goes back to the 1600's and is said to be responsible for the mutation of the color white and the long hair of cats.

Due to this scarcity, you would have to purchase a Turkish Angora cat instead of adopting one. So naturally, you are going to have to ask yourself some questions before deciding to invest in one of these animals to see if it is really worth the purchase. So, what are the pros and cons of owning one of these animals?

a. Cons
Let us start off with the cons of owning one of these animals. **Firstly, they are extremely expensive due to their rarity.** You should expect to put forth at least $800 or more to attain a quality pet kitten. You can also expect to be put on a waiting list for one of these animals as well.

Another con you should look out for does not necessarily have to do with owning but **the process of purchasing.** Due to the fact that these are such rare animals, a lot of cat breeders will claim to have these kittens when in fact they don't. Make sure to be on the look out for scam artists such as these. One way they may try to do this is by selling you cats without their papers.

The reasons why you should not buy an undocumented cat are obvious. These scammers may also try to give you fake papers for their kittens. Make sure to see that these papers are from the CFA, ACFA, or TICA. If they can't provide these documents, then it is not a Turkish Angora cat no matter what the breeder says.

b. Pros
Now for some of the pros of owning these animals:

Turkish Angora Cats are amazingly beautiful animals. – They are also available in a wide range of colors so you have many options when deciding on these animals. The Turkish Angora cat is available in black, blue, lilac, red, cream, cinnamon, tabby, white, red, caramel, and many more. This breed of cat also has fur that is amazing and silky to the touch. You will want to spend hours and hours petting this animal.

Along with being beautiful, these cats are also extremely smart and athletic. – This is what makes them so good at cat shows. Whenever it comes to the agility part of these cats, it shows the Turkish Angora cat usually excels.

The temperament of these cats can be described as social, affectionate, and playful. – This makes this cat ideal for a family type environment. A major perk of owning this animal is that although their coat is relatively long, this cat requires little grooming. They only require grooming at the moderate level.

Chapter 6: Basic Care of the Turkish Angora Cat

1) Introducing your kitten to your home

a. Settling in to the home

This may be an exciting time for you but cats take a longer time to adapt to the new environment. Cats are generally attached to their surroundings and change can be unsettling. Ensure your cat needs are met including easy access to food, water and a place to sleep. Others include a place to hide where the cat can sleep and hide away from the rest of the household. A raised area is advisable where your cat will sleep in a quiet environment.

Introduce the cat to the home by leaving doors open and making all rooms accessible. This will help the cat feel comfortable in his or her area. In contrast with this method, confining the cat to one room can help the cat get accustomed to the sounds and smells in the new home.

Place the litter box, bed, scratching post, food and water in a room with the cat. Surround the cat with things that smell familiar like a favorite bed, blanket or toys. Placing stuff that smell like you is another way that can make kittens more inclined to your scent.

Cat proof your home, tucking away electrical cords, ensure all windows have secure screens and remove any poisonous houseplants that may interfere with safety. If you plan on allowing your cat to go outside, make sure you keep him/her indoors for at least two weeks. This is mainly done to familiarize the cat with the home.

There are several things that the cat needs to get accustomed to before he/she decides to venture out into other spaces in the house. The smells and sounds around it are the first things that it must get accustomed to. There are several sounds that are new for it. Your voice, the sound of the telephone, the sound of your car starting in the driveway and all other sounds that seem quite ordinary to us are a big deal for your Turkish Angora.

There are several smells, like the smell of your furniture and carpeting that it must become familiar with. It must also get used to your smell. It is through these pieces of information that the cat analyses how safe the environment is.

If you are moving, all the above ways can work well. During the trip you can administer a sedative to ensure comfort throughout the journey in the cat carrier. Settling a new cat in your home is an essential part of ensuring they are comfortable with the environment. A cat that is not comfortable with their environment may run away from their new home. In this case, keep all doors and windows well shut to prevent the cat from running away.

b. Introducing the kitten to other pets
Introducing a new pet to your old pets at home can be challenging for every cat owner. It's important to have realistic expectations by recognizing and accepting the fact that you cannot force them to be friends. In this section we provide tips that work to increase your chances of success. Choosing a cat with the same activity level and personality is a good start. Another important aspect you need to know is the ages, especially because older cats may not appreciate the antiques of a kitten.

Cats are naturally territorial and can be unhappy with a newcomer. Cats hate change and a newcomer in the house can be a huge change. The cat may show displeasure by fighting with the other cat and marking their territory.

Some cats are more social than older animals that have never learnt to share their territory. In such a case, slow introductions may help to prevent fearful or aggressive behavior that may develop between the new cat and current cat. The slow introduction method takes from a few weeks to months and it needs a lot of patience on your part.

The confinement process includes allowing time for the newcomer to adjust to the new environment and situation. To do this, keep him/her in a small room with the litter box, food, water and toys for several days. Certain techniques have been successfully used to ensure the cat is comfortable in the new environment.

Feed your resident cat and the newcomer on opposite sides of the door. This way the cats can associate something enjoyable with each other's smells. Be careful not to put the food too close to each other in case they get too upset. In time, you can gradually move the dishes closer to the door until the cats can eat calmly, standing directly on either side.

Using a pet to improve interactions with the resident and newcomer cat is another way of introducing them. Tie a toy on either side of the door and hopefully they will start battling the toys around and even battling paws. Spend plenty of time with the new kitty in the confined room without ignoring the resident cat.

Smells are far more important than appearances. Swapping the blankets or beds that cats use and gently rubbing it across the cheek of the cats or underneath the food dish can help. When the pets finally meet, they will have familiar scents. Introducing a new pet to the other should be gradual so neither animal is afraid or aggressive. Face to face contact will tell you more in the direction of the new relationship. Mutual sniffing and grooming are signs that this process is on its way to success.

In a different case, the cats may show signs of aggression, which include flattened ears, growling, splitting or crouching. You can distract them by throwing a pillow to them to reduce the tension. Such standoff may take up to 24 hours. If the cats tend to fight repeatedly then you may need to start the process all over again. You can reduce the growing tension by having them share one litter box, keeping the resident cats' routine as it was before the newcomer and making sure they both have a safe place to escape.

c. Introducing kittens to children

According to the American academy of child & adolescent psychiatry, pets can:

Teach empathy and compassion

Provide love, loyalty and affection

Foster self-esteem

Promote physical activity

Teach responsibility

Provide valuable life lessons

Provide a connection to nature

Children are naturally drawn to cats but even so it's important to lay down some ground rules. An overzealous toddler could severely hurt a kitten. On the other hand, cat scratches and bites can pose serious health risks. It important to keep kids monitored during the interactions and to teach them about handling the cat with kindness and respect.

When toddlers become more mobile they may regard a cat as an animated stuffed toy. Toddlers operate at a cat's own level and move erratically, emitting giggles and squeals. It's important to teach them the simple rules of interactions with the cat to protect both the toddler and cat together unsupervised.

Teach your child the proper way to interact from stroking the cat to avoiding the more sensitive areas such as the tail, feet and belly. Explain that poking, squeezing or pulling fur, tails and ears are not okay. Toddlers are extremely sociable. Make sure the cat has safe escape perches and watch the body language of cats and children if they are worked up and separate them.

Older children are more reliable and are ready to start learning about how to care for the cat. Do not allow rough play, which may encourage the cat to use its teeth and claws by teaching your child ways to play with the cat using safe cat toys.

Teach the difference between teasing and playing. Model proper behavior by treating your cat with affection and respect at all times. Involve your children in caring for your cat; they can replenish food and water bowls, gently brush the cat or help in keeping litter pan clean. Teach them how to close the door, keeping them out of danger of going outside.

When it comes to associating and interacting with cats with children it's important to minimize such risks. It's important to bring your cat to regular cat checkups and fecal examinations. Ensure the cat is appropriately vaccinated and is free from infectious diseases. It's important to keep the cat indoors to minimize exposure to illnesses that cause organisms such as fleas or intestinal parasites. Wash your hands after handling the cat, discourage the child from kissing the cat or even allowing the cat to lick the child's face. Keeping litter pans clean will protect the curious toddler from accessing the litter pan.

2) Basic care and routine

An established routine is essential for any cat. Routines keep the day balanced and with an established one it's important for a new cat to develop into the routine. A routine may include playtime, feeding and bath time. As the owner, having a well established routine will help your cats to be well associated, especially if you own more than two.

A routine forms the basis of the security and comfort for the cat. Older cats tend to be less capable of adapting to changes; the slightest change, however small, comes with sudden reactions.

Cat routines can be good for bonding. Most cats are drawn to their owners because of being expectant of certain thing like brushing, ear cleaning and even baths. A cat with an established

49

routine makes it easy to detect when they are not feeling well. An ill cat may not necessarily use the same kind of routine they have established.

Some important cat routines for your cat are how often and when you play and exercise together, the consistency of diet, regular mealtimes, normal noise and activity levels in your household and morning and evening rituals for the family and the cat. Regular routines help you to plan a regular day on the weekly calendar to change the litter, buy cat food and groom your cat. A routine is an excellent way to be aware of the cat's health needs.

A Quick Note
It is tough bringing home a cat, as it can be risky when you are not certain of how it reacts with children as well as pets at home. The most common characteristic is aggression, which is prevalent among many cats. Naturally, cats are predators. Once the kittens stay behind with their mothers, there is a tendency for the kittens to be taught things like attacking or pouncing. This is merely an innate characteristic that is noticeable in all cats. Even with simple tools such as a roll of wool, the predator instinct is ever-present.

On the other hand, the Turkish Angora cat is absolutely unique with this aspect. Incidentally, it is accepting of all animals as well as pets in the house. Even with a dog around, the Turkish Angora cat is a highly co-existing character. Its ability to adapt easily with dogs is another beneficial feature. There should be no worries about the compatibility of a Turkish Angora kitten and a puppy, as they will develop a lasting relationship. The number of fights or brutal engagements between these cats and dogs is very minimal to rare, making them highly recommended as pet partners.

The compatibility of these Turkish Angora cats to kids is excellent. Thus, more parents prefer them for their children. Despite being extremely sensitive and gentle, it easily integrates itself and is most compatible with children. It is therefore natural to feel comfortable enough to leave the kids with your Turkish

Angora cat. Kids tend to enjoy the experience due to how playful the cat can get. The safety of the child is also assured.

The existence of another pet cat in the household may not always be a good thing. This is because some cat breeds do not go along well with the Turkish Angora. It would therefore be necessary to maintain a bit of caution to keep the peace. Its ability to dominate in situations will be evident eventually. No matter how well matched the cats may be, the Turkish Angora will always come out on top. The main cause for this will be the focus on seeking attention, rather than fighting for or sharing it.

Naturally, cats hold within them a social chain of command, commonly called a pecking order. The Turkish Angora follows the following command chain:

First, it listens to people.

Next, it listens to dogs.

Third, it listens to other cats.

Whatever the circumstance, the Turkish Angora will definitely be the most adaptable and friendly breed of cats available.

3) Astuteness

There is little in terms of doubt when in comes to the intelligence of the Turkish Angora cat breed. The ease with which one can impose training or tricks is amazing. This makes it a top breed in terms of teaching complex setups and games. The most common tricks are the parlor tricks. Other simple tasks involve toilet usage, obeying commands, and so on.

Another particular attribute that comes to attention is the curiosity of the Turkish Angora. The instances of peeking and prodding at 'exciting' places are numerous. As much as it may look ideal for their learning, it makes it almost impossible for you to institute brittle products as part of your interior home design. It would be disastrous to watch such a beauty being laid to waste by your Turkish Angora.

The immense appreciation of heightened area by the Turkish Angora cat means that you will expect to find them in the highest points of the house. Therefore, whenever you cannot locate them at the top of shelves or cupboards, it would only be fair to find them curled on the seats or your lap. They have no problem at all reaching these vantage points due to the extreme balance of the Turkish Angora cat bodies. They are also relatively swift, adding to that purpose. It is rare and almost impossible to find them under tables or sofas even when there are guests around.

There are no limitations as to which environment the Turkish Angora can thrive in well. This adaptation actualizes the claims of the sensitivity of these cats. No specific intent is made to stick to one person as they appreciate everyone gracefully. It may therefore be useless for you to try to steer the process of integration, since they are independent. This form of malleability makes the process of training it to follow a specific schedule much simpler.

The best way that the astute Turkish Angora cat learns most of its tricks is by observation. The sense of observance means that they can do intelligent tasks including opening doors. Without breaking a sweat, they will let themselves into a room by purposely turning the knobs. It will depend on you to lock them out of those rooms you may consider dangerous or sensitive. There are various features that define how intelligent they are, and with continuous hybridization, there is no limit to the functions they perform.

Being the owner of such an intelligent breed in the form of a Turkish Angora cat comes with unique benefits. The days of dull moments in the household are definitely gone with such a pet companion as a cat.

4) The Most Charming Cat

For the stay-at-home individual, the Turkish Angora breed is definitely the choice for you. Admirably social and active, it forms a good companion. Its beauty is just a portion of its antics to attract your attention. Be assured they will not be annoying, but rather entertaining and lovely.

The manner in which he or she quickly understands what pleases the owner makes it simpler because the actions will come very often. The best example is showing in the chasing of a roll of thread. The family also matters, with a constant input to please everyone. With the consistent entertainment, it will be difficult for you to take your attention off the cat.

The instances with in the cat will remain in a bored state are quite few, as they have a way of keeping themselves entertained. There is a huge momentum in its actions, with a natural demand to keep the social interaction by constantly creating play.

It is natural to lose interest in such antics after some time, but this does not mean you should grow impatient. So, what is the right reaction from a pet owner? Foremost, expect a clear expression of dissatisfaction from the Turkish Angora cat when that interest lacks. They definitely are not annoying or noisy, but rather vocal.

Nature demands of them to be sensitive, with a unique response to such instances. The response may be exceptionally shrill. Depending on the situation, the Turkish Angora will call or purr at various intensities. For example, after coming home, the typical reaction will be excitement purrs and following you around wherever you choose to go.

The Turkish Angora cat has sincere affection towards its owner, something that any individual would find welcoming and a sure sense of loyalty. They also enjoy the company, play and love that come with it. The most interesting bit is the manner in which it will react to an individual's temperament.

It's opposite reactions to sadness and feelings of frustration will often prove beneficial and rehabilitating to the owner. Otherwise, it is important to note that there is no option for it to abandon you.

Chapter 7: Synopsis of the Turkish Angora Cat Character

For easier understanding of the true character of this cat, the listing below will undoubtedly be of help. The rating of each attribute is out of five. The results here are an average of the response given by most Turkish Angora owners. It is thus upon you to choose it over other cats breeds.

Character attribute	Rating
Fondness towards Owner	5/5
Malleability	5/5
Playfulness	5/5
Congruency with Other Cats	3/5
Congruency with Dogs	4/5
Congruency with Children	4/5
Intelligence	5/5

Connecting with the Turkish Angora

There is a list of small to large tasks to engage your cat in as soon as it arrives. This is to create an atmosphere of understanding and getting to know you and its new environment so everyone in the room will be happy with what is happening.

a. The First Few Hours

Attempt to reach and cuddle the cat for its first feel of you. This is sometimes necessary if it feels nervous and comes to you.
Regular visits to the cat are recommended to build on trust.
Calling out to the cat in a soft voice while sitting in a low position would be more appealing and a better chance at bonding. Spacing the number of times you leave him/her alone in a room is fundamental too. The actual recognition may take a while, and as the owner, you are not expected to lose your patience. Allow time for proper recognition to take place.

Visits by children in your home or family should be in the company of an older individual. This may be limited to the first few days of the introduction into the family. The excitement from kids during such periods may be overwhelming, leading to slight injuries to them if they unsettle it. There should be adequate supervision at all times.

b. Create time for your cat

The Turkish Angora adores attention. There is a likelihood of the Turkish Angora feeling depressed if he or she feels less attended to. It is therefore proper to create time for them. It may not necessarily involve any sort of play, but rather having your presence felt in that room. In the case where there is more than one person in that home, the visits should come in turns to offer more options and improve on its co-existence with multiple persons. Remain in the room as long as possible to create some form of association.

c. Playtime

Through his or her (the Turkish Angora cat's) behavior, it is possible to find out whether there is a connection. The most common sign is to experience less hiding from the cat. The only way that they would want to show they are ready for you is by rubbing off their scent on you. This slowly begins with occasional rubs against your legs. This affectionate nature may not be met with a similar response if you try to touch them.

Employing toys is a nice way of initiating real contact with the cat. The best toy that evidently works is the use of a string or a shoelace. By running it along the floor, you tempt the predatory instinct in the cat to pounce on it. The cat will thus find it difficult not to play along. Immediately, the surroundings are clear and there is a clear connection building, there should be obvious fuss and endless play with you.

d. Special Circumstances

The heaviest challenge lies with the owner while trying to establish that bond. Whether there is a child or another pet in the house, it should be your task to intelligently introduce them to the cat. The methods will vary too. There is a certain model the Turkish Angora operates on, with the unique situation involving a grown cat. As described before, those steps can ensure a smooth transition in the bonding process. Making the process as comfortable as possible is recommendable.

Chapter 8: When a Turkish Angora is Pregnant

1) Reaching Puberty

When a male cat reaches puberty, he is known as a Tom. On the other hand, a female cat that hits puberty is known as the queen. Puberty in male cats sets in when they are about 6 or 9 months old. Breeding a male cat is only a good idea if the litter that he came from was healthy and was of a good size. His mother should not have had any complications while giving birth. You can ask your breeder for this information before you buy your cat.

The female cat will experience multiple cycles of heat during the breeding season. This season usually starts in January or February and continues until October or November. The temperature during this season and the ration between light and dark hours will play a significant role in your cat's heat cycle.

A female cat is ready to bear kittens at the age of 7 to 9 months. She will remain fertile for at least 9 years after she hits puberty. Only if your female cat comes from a healthy litter and a healthy mother should you consider breeding as a good option. You can have your cat tested for the possibility of genetic disorders and illnesses to understand how safe or reasonable it is to choose the option of breeding.

Most female cats will show obvious signs before the actual heat sets in. You will see her roll around on the floor, rub herself against objects and also meow persistently. However, she will not allow a tom to mount her. This is not a sign of pain as most owners presume. It is just your cat's hormones raging.

This heat cycle should last for about 8 days. The interval between one heat cycle and another is usually about 10 days. So expect your cat to exhibit this behavior at least twice a month during the breeding season.

The hormonal changes that take place in the cat's body in this period are tremendous. While estrogen causes the onset of the heat cycle, progesterone takes over when she is pregnant. As the level of estrogen increases, the heat cycle will intensify. Once the level of estrogen drops, the heat cycle ends. This rise and fall of estrogen will only end when she is mated.

2) Finding the Right Mate

Cats are extremely sensitive creatures. Most often, they will be able to choose their own mates when you take them to the breeder. If your cat has not been neutered or spayed, make sure you take them to a good breeder, especially with a pedigree like the Turkish Angora.

For Turkish Angora cats, it is not necessary for you to pick another Turkish Angora for mating. You can even outcross the cat with an American or British Short hair or a Burmese cat. Of course, if the goal is to achieve the same physical characteristics as the real Turkish Angora, a pure parent breed is recommended.

You must always take a queen to the tom for breeding, as she will not be too sensitive to these environmental changes during the mating process. The actual mating does not last for more than 4 minutes. Once this is over, the queen will break free by striking the male with her paw and turning away. The after reaction of the female is just cleaning herself after rolling and thrashing for a while. The after reaction may last up to 9 minutes.

If you are interested in producing a litter, you may have to allow your cat to be mated multiple times. With a single mating, there are only 50% chances of your cat getting pregnant. Studies show that female cats will allow up to 30 matings at intervals of 5 minutes.

One interesting fact about cats in general is that while each kitten has one father, the fathers of the kittens in a single litter may not have the same father. This is true because of the multiple mating processes. As a result, your litter may have several varieties of kitten, depending upon the cats that your queen has mated with.

If your cat is pregnant, you will see the apparent abdomen size by the 16th day of pregnancy. If you are not experienced with cats, an ultrasound can help you decide if your cat is pregnant or not. There is an easy way to check if your cat is pregnant or not. If the uterus feels stringy, it means that your cat might be pregnant. By the 20th day of pregnancy, you can actually feel the kitten fetuses in the abdomen of the queen when she is relaxed.

Besides checking for pregnancy, ultrasound is also a useful tool to check if the development of the fetuses is normal. You can perform an ultrasound from the 26th day of pregnancy until the end of pregnancy. Enlargement and a pinkish tinge of the mammary glands will be observed as the pregnancy progresses. Pregnancy may last for about 69 days.

3) Important Tips and Guidelines

The pregnancy period is a very delicate one. You must ensure that you take the best care of your Turkish Angora to have a healthy litter and also a safe delivery. Here are a few things to keep in mind while caring for a pregnant cat:

Morning sickness is common in cats. Your vet will be able to provide you with assistance if this persists.

Your pregnant cat may also reduce her food consumption by the third week of pregnancy.

Overfeeding and weight gain during pregnancy can lead to complications during labor.

The food that you give your queen must be highly nutritious. Protein and calcium are a must. However, never provide any supplements unless recommended by a vet.

Your cat must be kept indoors during the last 15 days of pregnancy. This helps you ensure that she does not give birth elsewhere.

During your cat's pregnancy, you must make sure that you visit the vet regularly. The most important time for your veterinarian visit is during the last two weeks of pregnancy.

4) Is my Turkish Angora in Labor?

There are some sure shot signs that will tell you if your beautiful Turkish Angora cat is ready to give birth. Here are some signs that you must look out for:

Your cat will begin to nest.

Her body temperature will drop to about 99 F.

She will start lactating.

Her appetite will reduce.

She will show extreme behaviors. She will either become extremely affectionate or she will just become entirely reclusive.

5) Preparing for Birth

The one phase where you will experience maximum anxiety is when your Turkish Angora actually gets ready to give birth. If you are not prepared, you will just end up fumbling and jeopardizing the health of your kitty. Here are some things that you must keep in handy when your cat is in the last two weeks of her pregnancy:

A sturdy cardboard box or a kittening box available at pet stores.

Surgical gloves.

A syringe or eyedropper to remove secretions from the nose and mouth.

Cotton thread or Dental floss for the umbilical cord ties.

Antiseptic for the umbilical stumps.

Scissors.

Clean and fresh towels.

The vet's number.

Milk replacer for kittens.

Emergency contact numbers.

Now, all you need to do is prepare for the actual birth. When your cat is in the last week of her pregnancy, place the kittening box in a quiet spot. This spot should be warm and completely draft free. Place your cat's favorite blanket and some toys in this box to encourage her to sleep there.

The bedding that you choose for this kittening box should be comfortable for the kittens and shouldn't snag their claws. This bedding must be changed regularly after the birth of the kittens.

6) Danger signs

In case you observe one or more of the following symptoms, make sure you call your vet right away:

Lack of appetite in your queen for 24 hours or more

The temperature is high and continues to stay elevated

She becomes lethargic

She has unpleasant smelling discharge from her vagina

These are signs that something might have gone wrong during the delivery. They also indicate postnatal stress in your cat and must be treated at the earliest.

7) Things you must not do during pregnancy

Never use any flea powder or medicine without consulting your doctor first.

Do not allow your Turkish Angora to take any medication without a valid prescription.

Do not use antiseptics suitable for humans. These products, although mild on our skin, may burn your cat's delicate skin.

Avoid handling the kittens too much. There are chances that your cat will disown or even kill the kittens if intruders threaten them. Allow the kittens and the mother to bond.

Do not allow your cat to roam around. Cats can get pregnant within 2 weeks of delivery. So keep her in confinement for a while.

Do not de-sex your cat until after 7 weeks of the kittens' birth.

Taking care of a pregnant cat is a huge responsibility. If you are not sure of how to go about it, you can look for a shelter or a veterinary hospital where the cats will be taken care of until the kittens are born. Once you have the kittens, you can decide if you want to keep them in your home or find them another loving home to live in.

Chapter 9: Training the Turkish Angora

A well-trained cat is easy to maintain and look after. An ill-mannered cat can stress the owner, for example, litter box training an untrained cat may end up in a mess. A well-trained cat is able to use the litter box, keeping the house clean.

The elegance and grace of this intelligent, athletic breed with the super silky flowing coat is what makes the Turkish Angora attract people who love pets that love them. Turkish Angoras are adorable and more social and can make a fantastic companion as they enjoy interacting with their human family as with other cats.

Turkish Angoras are very smart and engaging in lifting our spirit but so silly if not trained on their boundaries as they jump and climb everywhere and anywhere they please. They like seeking attention anyway. Unlike dogs that relax pretty much on the floor, these silly felines can jump from the top of doors to the floor in the room and then to the kitchen as if they want to help you do the dishes. This is the reason why it is important to train and manage your cat to fit your personal needs.

The Turkish Angora is trainable in different areas including litter box training. Here we will discuss some of the main tips you can use for litter box training, leash training and teaching tricks.

1) Litter box training

Buy a litter box that will be comfortable for the cat. Buy litter that is not too rough for the cat as this may discourage the cat. There are different types of litter to choose from, which are generally fine for all cats. Perfumed litter and scoopable litter are some of the litter available in general stores. As the cat grows older, you will need to switch litters, especially if it starts eating the litter. Kittens can become ill from ingesting large quantities of litter; those made from clay are especially lethal to any aged cat.

Cats have a natural instinct to eliminate in sand or soil. With kittens, they learn mainly from observing their mother. If you have a new kitten, they will need guidance on where to eliminate and use of the litter boxes. Training on litter can be done with a kitten as young as 3 weeks to 4 weeks of age.

It is important to make sure your kitten knows the location of the litter box in her new surroundings. Ensure the litter box is not placed in a noisy area or places with high traffic like the kitchen, as cats enjoy their privacy. Introducing them to the litter box will be done manually by placing the kitten in the litter box for them to get used to it. Teach the kitten how to scratch on the litter by placing the front paws inside; this will give her confidence.

Place the cat in the litter box at different times when they would normally go to the bathroom in the morning, after meals, playing and waking up from their nap. Most cats will make the adjustments to a new litter box without any problems.

When accidents happen, do not scold or yell at the cat; instead, clean up the accident with an enzyme cleaner to remove stains and odors. Yelling and scolding will end up confusing your cat, which may slow down the litter box training. If you notice more accidents with a bout of diarrhea, consult your veterinarian to rule out any foreseen medical problems.

You should provide one litter box per cat plus one extra. Some cats prefer to use one litter box to urinate and another to defecate in. It may seem excessive to have more than one litter but cats can be choosy creature, which may increase the chances of small accidents in the house.

Choosing the right size of litter box is essential. Kittens require a smaller size that they can be able to climb into without much effort. Self-cleaning litter boxes are also available, which save on clean up time, though some are noisy. Hooded box concentrates odor and should be cleaned daily.

Cleanliness is an important factor for the cats and they may avoid a litter box that is not clean. Scoop the litter box at least once per day and wash the litter box and change the litter once a week. Keep off strong smelling disinfectants that may affect the cat's superior sense of smell. Training a new cat or kitten how to use a litter box is not an easy thing, so reward them with treats when they get it right and see the difference.

Training a cat requires much patience and perseverance to bring about performance and tricks. It is advisable for you to adapt a kitten as young as three months old and start training him/her so as to achieve satisfying results in performance. Upon acquiring your kitten, don't allow it full run of the house. Try to contain him/her to one room, preferably the one you spend most of your time in, so that you can watch over it.

Immediately carry it without delay to the litter box if your kitten accidentally pees or poops where not needed.

Cats and kittens don't like using heavily soiled litter boxes, so ensure that the litter box is clean. You can thoroughly wash the litter box once a week.

Finally, litter training requires patience as the cat is learning a new thing. Be patient and not pushy during this process. For the new cat, comfort is important and for them it may take longer. The Turkish Angora cat is one of the most intelligent cat breeds and learning how to use the litter box will be an easy process.

2) Leash training

Teaching a cat to walk on a harness and leash is a great way to let your cat enjoy the outdoors while ensuring they are safe. Outdoor walks can reduce obesity and boredom-related behavior that develops due to under exercise. Because cats may easily escape a collar, it's not a safe alternative. Patience is a virtue when strapping the cat to a harness. Leash training, just like other training related to pet animals, will take time. Here we will discuss the process of leash training.

a. Equipment

A good harness must be well fitted for the cat, designed for cats and must be comfortable for the cat to wear. It should be practical for the cat and lightweight - made of either cloth or nylon. Chain and leather leashes are too heavy for a cat. Attach the leash with a collar identification tag.

Leave the harness near the cat's food or favorite sleeping spot for several days. This will give the cat feelings of contentment when they see the leash. Another way is to let the cat sniff the harness by holding it close to them.

b. Acclimating the cat to the leash

This process needs to be a slow process, as rushing may cause the cat to shy away from wearing the harness. Place the harness on the cat, which is best done when the cat is relaxed to avoid any type of agitation. As you hold the harness against the cat's neck, offer treats as you lay the harness and do so as it sniffs the treat too.

If your cat does not appreciate being held or restrained, get the cat used to handling. You can do this by keeping a favorite toy close by and holding it firmly but gently for a few seconds. Use soft praises while holding it and giving him/her treats. Repeat this exercise often for several days while practicing handling the cat's legs and feet.

Drape the harness over the cat's shoulders and down his/her chest between his/her front legs. Introduce this new feeling as the cat is sniffing and eating treats, work until you can snap the harness on it over his/her neck and shoulder area between his/her front legs, continuing to distract with treats.

Put the harness on the cat but do not attach the leash immediately. While distracting the cat with treats, adjust the harness to fit the cat, making sure only two fingers can fit between the cat and harness. Repeat this daily, and as the cat seems more relaxed, increase the time when the harness is on. Remove the harness if the cat seems upset.

Now it's time to attach the leash. Place your cat in an empty room, making sure nothing can snag the leash. Distract your cat with treats and as it walks around the room be sure to keep an eye for anything that may snag, as this may scare it. Repeat this for several days until the cat becomes comfortable.

After realizing the cat is comfortable and relaxed with the leash while dragging it, slowly and gently hold the leash, not pulling, while it walks around the house. Praise it often and give treats and continue practicing this step for several days.

c. Going outside

After the successful leash training process, you may proceed to go with the cat outside. However, you can also direct the cat as he/she walks around the house. When you're outside it may be easier to direct the cat to the direction you want.

Once you're outside, the excitement of the outdoors may overwhelm your cat. You can encourage the cat to walk along with you by using a sweet, soft voice, dropping a treat while you're walking, and applying pressure on the leash if the cat goes a different direction. Keep it close to avoid any accidents.

Do not leave the leash on the cat tied to something while you are away, as the cat may get tangled and get hurt.

3) Teaching the cat tricks

Cats are intelligent and capable of being taught new tricks. It is advisable to start teaching tricks to kittens because they are more energetic at that time. A cat can learn different tricks from dancing, standing, clapping and many more. In this Chapter, we discuss some of the tips that have stood out and are successful.

Although kittens are most recommended for teaching new tricks, here we explore options on how to train older cats new tricks. For those who have adopted or bought older cats, this section will be an important part in terms of interactions.

Communication

Animal behaviorist experts say that cats can be trained by a pattern of reinforced treats. In psychology, the term used is conditioned response. Certain behavior patterns can be established in this theory, like when cats respond to the opening of a can or even the sound of clapping on their food plate. Training your cat will also depend on how well you communicate with each other. Engaging your cat in conversation on a daily basis is the fastest way to teach your cat the tune of your voice.

Body language

Cats communicate mostly through their body language and it's important to be able to recognize the meaning of each move. This can include – tail position, reading the eyes, the ears and leg rubbing – all these are communication patterns cats use.

The tail position of a cat can tell you so much about their emotions. The tail of the cat acts as a mood barometer and provides balance for the cat. You may notice at times the tail of the cat is held loosely upright when walking, this shows confidence and contentment.

If you find your cat flicking its tail upright in your direction, it is giving you a warm greeting. If it whips it from side to side or thumps it on the floor, it means he/she is agitated or angry, so find out what is making it angry. If the cat puffs the tail, he/she may be spooked by something or someone and is receptive by calming her down.

Read the eyes when a cat looks at you. If the eyes are dilated, it means he/she is nervous or agitated and requires some space. The eyes of a cat are the most stunning features and they communicate a lot of emotion. A cat's ears move when the cat is being receptive and you will notice that the ears look forward and slightly outward. A ready to fight cat flattens its ears against its head.

When you find your cat rubbing against your legs or brushing its cheekbone against your hand, it means that he/she is marking you. It sets a sense of belonging to the part of the cat, a type of feline flattery. In some ways, it may be translated as marking its territory against other animals, either outside or within the household.

Sounds

Different sounds can also be translated into communication. These sounds include the meow, purr, chirp and trill. Meow sounds may be a sign of demanding something. This could be food or daily walks, it depends on the need at that particular time.

The purr sound happens when they are receiving an end message. It may also be due to the discomfort of visiting the veterinary clinic. Cats purr with their mouths closed. The chirp sound happens when they see prey or flies in the house. They may make this noise when they see certain animals such as birds, squirrels and other small creatures.

A trill is between a meow and purr and is a greeting. Other sounds you will hear from your cat include growling, chattering, yowling, hissing and wailing. It will be important to master these noises for efficient communication with your cat.

4) Training a cat to learn new tricks

After learning about the different communication strategies that you can relate to, now you can start teaching your new pet new tricks. Tricks include sitting up, come here, jump, and shake hands and waving. All this will require adequate communication between you and your cat.

Bonding with your cat will be cemented during this period of training. One thing you need to understand is the aspect of appraisal by use of treats. Cats love appreciation. By doing so, you are motivating it.

The Turkish Angora is an intelligent cat and is a fast learner when it comes to learning new tricks. Its playful nature will provide a better atmosphere of learning new tricks. Most of the showcased cats in cat shows go through intensive training.

Animal psychologists advise owners to train their cats for a few minutes during the day. Training your cat has important benefits like stimulating the body and mind, keeping your cat healthy. Spending time together will strengthen your bond. Here are some helpful tips to help you as you teach your cat new tricks.

Use tasty treats. By identifying your cat's favorite treat, you can follow these basic steps of positive reinforcement training. First you have to get the attention of your cat by holding the treat to your cat's nose.

Move it in different directions on its face and chin and as he/she follows your movements, you will notice the butt will go down. When its bottom hits the floor, praise your cat and offer the treat. Repeat this several times if your cat does not completely hit the floor. Repetition is the best way to remind your cat what you have already taught it.

Using a Clicker

Clicker training is considered the easiest way to train cats some new tricks. The first goal in clicker training is to establish a simple form of communication between the trainer and the cat. It allows the cat to understand what specific noises are saying. This allows you as the trainer to pick just about anything the cat does and encourage it to repeat the same thing or do it on command.

Clicker training can also be efficiently used during litter box training. When the cat uses the litter box in the correct way, use the clicker to appreciate and encourage it to do it again. Although there are many different clickers on the market, one can use a pen that resembles the same noise. Even in cat training, practice makes perfect.

Don't punish

Cats do not respond well to punishment. They run away rather than learning from their behavior. Depending on the cat's temperament, punishment can frighten your cat to the extent that it hides away from you and your family members. Punishment may cause and alleviate stress levels in your cat, which in some cases may trickle down to their normal cat behaviors. Eliminating outside the litter box or even compulsive grooming are some of the signs of a stressed cat.

Cats are responsive and relate to different commands. A cat that is taught to follow your voice can be easily trained to do simple tricks. Teach the cat to sit by positioning it in a sitting position; repeat this until the cat understands the sit down command. Use treats for this trick, as this will help motivate the cat to respond to the command much more easily.

Shake a hand- take the paw of your cat and shake it while saying your chosen command, such as shake hands. Repeat this exercise and soon the cat will respond lovingly to your paw shake. The paw shake is a great way to show off to your visitors.

Provide a safe environment when teaching new tricks as cats respond to distractions. This may eventually slow the process of teaching new tricks to your cat. A well-trained cat is enjoyable to have and will amaze you with newfound tricks each time.

Cats do most things on their own but again they are quick learners. Just like dogs, cats are trained to sit, dance and even shake their paws. In order to train your cat to learn these tricks, first of all, identify your cat's personality and energy level. Most importantly, have some fun in it and have the tricks that will motivate your cat to continue training because if the cat gets frustrated, he/she won't continue and definitely you wouldn't achieve your goal.

Tricks to get your cat to sit well – Hold a treat above your cat's head and mouth and then command him/her to sit down so that all four paws and bottom are on the floor. As it tries to struggle to eat the treat, place the back of your hand on its head to guide him/her down so that he/she gains balance and after that, give him/her the treat to eat. Doing this repeatedly will get your Turkish Angora to understand when you say "sit down".

Shake a hand- take the paw of your cat and shake it while saying your chosen command, such as shake hands. Repeat this exercise and soon the cat will respond lovingly to your paw shake. The paw shake is a great way to show off to your visitors.

Jumping and dancing – Hold the treat some inches above his/her mouth and say "jump" or put the treat on a toothpick or stick and hold the stick vertically in front of your cat's face and tell it to get it. As the cat tries to sniff the treat, take it away from him/her. When he/she can no longer stand bipedal or falls on the floor, praise him/her and give the treat so that he/she feels rewarded for the efforts made.

Roll over – This is the trick to train your cat to lie down. First place your cat on a table and hold the treat under the table. Guide your cat to lie down by saying the command "lie down", then once your cat can follow the command, take the treat and stand up over its head and command it to roll. This is not easy and so your cat might need some time to learn this trick.

Rewarding is the most motivating factor while training your cat. If you are using food and your cat does not respond, maybe he/she is not hungry. Try another tactic like praising or patting and this can work. Do the training session on a regular basis so that your cat can get used to and learn the tricks quickly.

Choosing the right method will depend on your relationship with your cat. In many instances, cats with a healthy relationship with the owner are found to be more receptive to commands. As we discussed above, the aspect of communication between you and the cat are important for developing a bond between you.

In conclusion, training a cat is an easy task by using the simple principles. Whether it's litter box training, leash training and teaching new tricks, communication is an important aspect. As the cat owner you need to understand the cat's temperament. This will go a long way in your relationship.

Does your cat need a friend? Research shows that cats that grow up in pairs are the happiest. So, if you want to get your cat a companion, you can ask your breeder for the most suitable option.

How pet friendly is your home? A Turkish Angora is the perfect apartment cat. So even if you live in an apartment, it will not really matter. However, if there are any restrictions with respect to keeping pets in your apartment, you must be aware of it. In addition to that you must make sure that you also have access to pet stores and vets in the area that you live in. If you feel that your home is inconvenient for your pet, you might want to rethink the option of owning a cat.

Your Lifestyle: If you feel like your Turkish Angora will not have enough company while it is at home, do not even think of purchasing a cat. Turkish Angoras crave attention and can have several health complications if they are not given ample love and affection.

Once all these issues have been sorted, you can prepare your home for the Turkish Angora. Several Turkish Angoras require a home. You can consider the option of adopting. However, before you do, here are some things that you must be able to provide your adopted pet with:

Necessary care in case of reported abuse

Vet assistance if it is ill or old

A separate room or enclosure to protect him/her and other pets at home

Constant care to help it adapt

The necessary nutrition if he/she has health issues.

If you are confident of being able to provide all of the above, adoption is the noblest thing that you can do for your pet. Give him/her a loving home where it will be able to learn to live a life of dignity and happiness.

Chapter 10: Grooming the Turkish Angora

Cat grooming is a pro job. Professional expertise can only ensure that the cats are hygienically perfect and look beautiful too. There can be many diseases and infections that can be caused by the fur of the cat. Therefore, the owners of the cats should use state of the art methodologies to clean and groom their cats. There are professional cat grooming centers that can do the job more conveniently and quickly for you.

The owners of the cats can also groom their cats, provided they have the required knowledge and equipment to groom, clean and beautify their cats. As most of the owners love their cats to bits, they prefer to groom their cats by themselves. The Turkish Angora cat is one of the most loved breeds of cats and requires special care and techniques in order to groom it.

Turkish Angora cats come with short fur that is the deepest shade of black. The coat of a Turkish Angora has a very leathery appearance. For a cat whose coat is its trademark, it would not be too surprising if grooming was expensive and time consuming.

What makes the Turkish Angora even more special is the fact that its grooming requirements are almost zero. This is one of the easiest to maintain breeds of cat. All you need to worry about is overall hygiene and your Turkish Angora will look more beautiful by the day.

Grooming is not an essential part of owning a Turkish Angora Cat. However, there are several reasons besides the physical appearance of your pet to ensure that you include grooming sessions. You accomplish five things by grooming your Turkish Angora:

You get to dedicate time to spend with your cat.

You help to maintain the health of the cat by removing loose hairs and debris that the cat may choke on in the process of pruning itself.

You are able to keep an eye out for infections, cuts and other skin disorders.

Your cat's coat is your responsibility. You can maintain the lustrous black coat of the Turkish Angora by bathing, brushing and cleaning the coat on a scheduled basis.

You can take care of your own belongings and prevent injuries to people by maintaining the claws of your Turkish Angora.

If you are not sure of how to go about the grooming process, several professionals are willing to help you with it. You can approach cat-grooming specialists and have maintenance contracts according to your convenience. Most of them will be specialized in dealing with cats and can be trusted to give your kitty the best.

1) Benefits of Grooming a Turkish Angora cat

There are several benefits associated with grooming Turkish Angora cats. It does not only beautify the cat but also looks after a lot of health and care issues related to the cats. Here is a brief list of the benefits associated with the grooming of Turkish Angora cats:

- Grooming of the cats helps in improving the muscles tones.

- It helps to stimulate the skin, which in return produces oil. The oil produced gives healthy shine to the coat of the Turkish Angora cat.

- Turkish Angora cats can remove a lot of hairs every time they are groomed. If you groom your Turkish Angora cat on daily basis, especially when your cat is malting, then you can remove the majority of loose hairs from the coat of the cat.

- This practice also helps in preventing the formation of hairballs on the coat of the cat. If you do not groom your cat on a regular basis, then it can lead to certain severe problems like forming hairballs on the fur, which can catch more and more germs and bacteria.

- The grooming session also gibes the master or the attendant to have a close physical look at the cat. Sometimes, there can be serious injuries or infection, which is not noticed in the normal routine until they are taken for a grooming session.

- In the grooming session, the attendant can have a close look at the overall body including ears, eyes, nose, and mouth, ear mites, checking for fleas, or any formation of lumps or bumps on the body of the cat.

- The grooming session can be very therapeutic for the concerned parties, the cat and the attendant. Both the attendant and the cat can develop a good bonding between them.

Cats can be a difficult animal to groom for the first time. There is a need to develop a good bonding between the two concerned parties. The good bonding can be developed with the newly born kitten. It is a natural tendency of the new kitten that it always responds in a positive way to any love or affection shown towards it. Once the cat matures or a new master adopts it, then it can be a really daunting job to get accustomed with the new cat.

Turkish Angora cats especially have this tendency. In such circumstances, a nice and friendly grooming session can be an excellent means to developing a good relationship between the master and his/her cat. The first grooming session is the most important when either the cat or the master should strive to develop a bonding.

If both of them fail the first time in developing an understanding, then it can get extremely difficult to carry on a smooth grooming session the next time. Any nasty surprises from either of the two could lead to a bad relationship, which can be extremely difficult to minimize if the attendant does not handle things very well.

2) Equipment needed for grooming a cat

As cat grooming is a complex process, some sophisticated equipment is need. Here is some of the equipment needed for grooming the Turkish Angora or any other cat:

- Clippers

- Blades

- Combs

- Brushes

- Shampooing products

- Soaps

3) Handling and Safety Pointers

The health and safety of both the Turkish Angora cat and the person grooming is important. Dealing with cats or any kind of animals could lead to fatal injuries. Cat bites can be extremely painful and can have long lasting effects. It can cause certain fatal infections that can take time to cure or sometimes can get worse. Therefore, in order to groom a Turkish Angora cat, your safety should be the main concern.

Make sure you take all the safety precautions before beginning with the cleaning and grooming of your cat. The personality traits of both the cat and the person doing the grooming process should be carefully assessed. There are a lot of cat lovers that are also allergic to the fur of the cats. Therefore, they are highly advised wear gloves before starting the process. This would either eliminate or at least reduce any threat of catching any allergy from the cat.

Furthermore, the cats as well have some dodgy personality traits that can be of concern. They can have sharp nails or teeth, which can cause injuries to the person servicing the cat. Safety equipment like gloves or safety jackets is highly advised.

For the safety of the service provider, the Turkish Angora cat can also be equipped with safety equipment. The cat can be made to wear a mouth mask and small pads over its paws. This precautionary measure can significantly reduce the chances of any possibility of physical damage caused to the attendant or the service provider.

Cats of the Turkish Angora breed can have different temperaments. They have the tendency to get violent during their cleaning or grooming sessions. Some cats do not enjoy their grooming sessions and can attack. On the other hand, some Turkish Angora cats remain completely calm throughout the session.

You should try to divert the attention of violent cats. This can be presented with their most loved playing equipment while the attendant can easily carry on with the grooming job. The owner or master of the Turkish Angora cat is the best person to judge the traits and temperament of his/her cat. He/she knows when the cat gets violent and what activities can amuse it the most. He/she also has an idea of how to control the cat during the grooming session.

Therefore, if you are looking to get your cat groomed from a professional, make sure that you as the owner of the cat are also present throughout the session. It is true that the professionals should have all the tactics to control the cat, but the cat in a new environment like a cat-grooming parlor can easily get violent, especially when he/she does not see his/her master around.

Hygiene and sanitation of the Turkish Angora or any other cat is also of utmost consideration. Neglecting any of these aspects could lead to incurable diseases. Either the attendant doing the servicing of cats at home or a commercial cat-grooming center should carry on with the process while maintaining the required standards.

The equipment used should be properly sterilized before commencing the grooming session. It is also highly recommended that the equipment used once should be immediately sterilized after the grooming session and once before commencing with a new grooming session.

Furthermore, the same equipment should not be used for different animals, which are normally a major concern at the pets grooming centers. The reason for not mixing the grooming equipment is the different traits of different animals. The equipment used for washing should also be of top quality with no substandard goods. People who love their cats know very well how valuable their cat's skin is for them. Ordinary shampoo or bathing equipment could result in severe fur loss or can also cause the reduction in the quality of hair and its skin.

4) Can a Tranquilizer Work?

Sometimes a cat needs to be safely relaxed prior to grooming. It is therefore highly recommended to have the cats vaccinated with tranquilizing materials at their due times before grooming. Especially before going for a grooming session, special vaccinations can be injected that can assure the cat remains calm throughout the grooming session. The Turkish Angora cat is a popular breed, so special vaccinations are also available on the market to treat this breed of cats. It is advised always to mention the breed of your Turkish Angora cat before purchasing any vaccination product for them.

5) Types of Grooming for Turkish Angora Cats

The different kinds of grooming techniques are based on the coat or fur of the Turkish Angora cats. Both long and short-haired cats have different needs in grooming. Their fur is the most valuable part of their body by looks. Long hairs are groomed using brushes and combs suitable for long hair, which are also soft to the body and do not make any scratches on it.

The clippers and blades also vary for treating a small or a longhaired cat. The shampooing technique also has a different style for serving both types. Using any equipment that is not suitable for a particular type can damage its fur, can cause skin rashes and scratches and can result in a serious type of cat infection.

a. Grooming Shorthaired Turkish Angora Cats

Grooming a shorthaired Turkish Angora cat requires some special equipment like a fine-edged comb, a fine bristle hairbrush and a rubber pad for grooming, which can also be a special kind of mitten for the cats. The grooming session should be started when you are sure that the cat is feeling very relaxed and happy. Initially, you should look to groom your cat at least once per week.

Then you can increase the frequency once you develop a good bonding with your cat. For the first grooming session, use the flea comb only in order to check for flea excreta. The flea excreta are used to check the tiny dirt particles in the comb, which eventually turns red if a drop of water is dropped onto it. If you find that the dirt particles turn red with the drop of water, then you should immediately contact your veterinary doctor for further inspection and treatment of the problem.

You can also massage or move your fingers through the coat of the cat in order to loosen the dead hairs on the cat's body. The technique for massaging should be used against the hair growth of the cat's coat. Doing it this way ensures that the dead hairs are removed from the coat, which otherwise would not have been possible.

Gently brush the coat of the cat using the brush with the direction of the brush stroke going towards the tail of the cat. The given brush stroke should be long and should be started from the head of the cat and finish at the tail.

If you think that your cat can tolerate the bristle brush, then try using it. Just one stroke of the bristle brush will tell you whether to continue with this equipment or not. If it is not suitable, then the cat can become violent and restless and can make certain painful noises. A bristle brush is important as they can bring the deep loose hairs on the surface of the coat. The deep hairs are not easy to bring up on the skin by massaging or by using your hands.

When the deep dead hairs come to the surface, you can then use the special mitten or the glove to remove those loose, dead hairs off the coat. The hands can also remove those loose hairs; but using the rubber glove or mittens gives the coat a shiny finish. The grooming session should be kept as short or as long as the cat is comfortable with. If you think that the cat is getting uncomfortable, then just finish the session.

b. Grooming Longhaired Turkish Angora Cats
In order to groom a longhaired Turkish cat, the first equipment you need is a wide-spiked comb and a rubber pad or a rubber mitten. The grooming frequency of longhaired cats should be a lot more than the shorthaired cats for the obvious reasons. Longhaired cats ideally should be groomed every day for keeping everything in order but with very careful attention, considering the tolerance level and the temperament of the cat.

The time spent on the cat should again be very reasonable, in which the cats show no sign of discomfort. For longhaired cats too, choose the time for the grooming session when the cat is properly fed, relaxed and happy. Begin by massaging the body with your hands going against the direction of the hair growth.

As the dead hairs are removed, then check for flea excreta as discussed for the shorthaired cats and follow the same procedure. Use the brush by giving strokes from the head to tail of the cat and remove any loose, dead hairs. Take particular care while brushing the area under the cat's armpits, as the skin here is very fine and sensitive. Do not use scissors to cut any hair knots or mats.

There is a large range of brushes and combs that you can choose from for your cat. The Turkish Angora cat, however, does not require a fancy brush, as its fur is short and extremely easy to comb.

You can get your Turkish Angora a slick brush that has steel bristles. These brushes not only keep the fur neat, they also massage the skin of your cat. All types of cats, especially the Turkish Angora, love this type of brushing action.

You can also bring home grooming pads and gloves made of rubber. You can remove any dead hair for the short coat of your beautiful Turkish Angora. You can even use flea combs to serve this purpose.

6) How to Brush the Fur of your Turkish Angora

Brushing may seem like a very ordinary task. However, if done right, the benefits of brushing your Turkish Angora cat will be multiplied. If you look up any blog or book with Turkish Angora cat information, brushing is suggested as a great grooming technique. Here is how you can brush the fur of your Turkish Angora, the 'right' way.

Make sure all the strokes are even and in the direction of the fur. This will help eliminate the loose hairs and actually massage the cat's body.

Using a cat hairbrush, brush off all the loose hairs for your cat's body.

You can even use your grooming gloves to get rid of any debris that is visible on your cat's coat.

Your cat's skin consists of several natural oils. Massaging the body thoroughly after brushing will help distribute this oil evenly across the cat's body to produce healthier and shiner fur.

Your cat's skin is very thin. Make sure that the bristles of the brush are not too sharp. You must also ensure that you do not apply too much pressure while brushing the fur. It can cause cuts and bruises more easily in a shorthaired cat like the Turkish Angora.

7) Trimming the Nails of the Turkish Angora cat

Several tools can be used to trim the nails of the cat. You can easily use a regular human finger nail cutter to trim the nails of the cat. There is specialized equipment also available for the trimming of animal's nails such as a scissors or a guillotine. Just ensure that the tool is reasonably sharp.

A dull edge can crash the nails of the cat. The goal is to just trim the fine edges of the nails of the cat. Just ensure that there is enough light when you are performing the trimming of the cat's nails. This makes sure that the tool is used just at the intended portions and does not damage the whole nail or skin of the cat, which can get fatal.

A nail trimmer is the cheapest grooming tool that you can get for your cat. It will cost you under $10. This is a very simple tool to use. The reason most cat owners make use of these nail clippers is to ensure that the upholstery and furniture in the house is protected from the sharp claws of the cat.

There are several types of clippers that are available on the market. The safest ones are the cat claw scissors that come with blunt ends to protect the cat from cuts and clipping injuries.

Many pet owners think of declawing as a suitable grooming technique. This surgical procedure removes the claws of the cat entirely. Also known as onychectomy, this procedure involves the removal of the end bones of the cat's toes partly or entirely. This practice is very common in North America. However, because of the effects it has on the cat and its well-being, it is also considered animal cruelty in many parts of the world.

This practice is followed in order to prevent the cat from damaging furniture and property. Other pet owners also justify declawing a cat as a method of protecting other people from being scratched or hurt by their cat. In many apartments, people are not allowed to keep cats unless they are completely declawed.

It is quite certain that these people do not understand the seriousness of this procedure. It is not a way of keeping the nails trimmed or blunt. Medical surgery has untoward repercussions on the cat. The toenails of your cat are actually attached very closely to its bones.

Therefore, removing the claw is as good as amputating the toes of your cat. The period of recovery is extremely painful for the cat. There is also no guarantee that your beloved pet will recover entirely from this traumatic experience. For this reason, several European countries have strong laws against declawing cats.

The Turkish Angora Cat is very peaceful and pleasant by nature. With declawing, however, several owners swear by the fact that the personality of the cat changes. There are valid reasons to support this change in behavior and personality of the cat.

The biting frequency and strength increases in most cats. The only possible explanation for this is that when a cat loses one form of defense, it activates another.

House soiling is twice as common in declawed cats. Firstly, they become reluctant to walk and put pressure on their paws. In addition to that, severe cases like nerve dysfunction and even lameness renders the cat quite helpless.

Aggression is very common in cats post declawing. The pain makes them more defensive against people. In addition, the fact that you as the owner inflicted that pain upon it makes you less trustworthy in the eyes of the cat.

Almost 45% of cats that have been declawed are referred to vet teaching hospitals and cat schools to sort out behavioral issues. The change in behavior is more drastic if the cat has undergone tendonectomy in the process of being declawed. The repercussions of these behavior changes include relinquishing cats to shelters. For a cat like the Turkish Angora, which is so attached to people, this experience is extremely traumatic.

8) Dental Care

Dental Care is very important for cats. It is almost as important as it is in humans. The truth is that cats tend to have huge amounts of tartar deposits on their teeth. This may result in gum damage and even tooth decay. Instead of taking your pet to the vet for cleaning procedures, you can simply keep a brushing kit to keep your cat's teeth in the best condition possible. If you do not maintain your cat's dental health, chances are that you will end up spending close to $500 on the anesthesia, antibiotics and other medicines required.

You will need to brush your cat's teeth regularly. You can get your cat used to having it's teeth brushed by first inserting your hands into its mouth, before using the toothbrush. Move it around as you would a toothbrush until the cat feels comfortable. Only then can you use the toothbrush to clean its teeth. You can buy pet toothpaste from most pet stores or vets, but please do not use human toothpaste.

9) Eye Care of the Turkish Angora cat

If you think that your Turkish Angora cat has excessive tear staining, then it is better to consult your veterinary doctor. In case they are reasonably short and have no medical conditions, then you can also use any of the commercial eye stain removal products for cats yourself. However, excretions from the eyes are generally signs of unhealthy eyes, so always consult a vet.

10) Ear Care of the Turkish Angora cat

The ears are also a pivotal organ of cats and should be given the utmost care for health and hygienic reasons. The attendant or the master should inspect the ears of their Turkish Angora cat every week. Unattended ears can result in the development of ear-mites, bacterial infections, allergies and yeast infections inside the ears. Regular inspection and then cleaning of the ears can make sure that the cat is safe from such allergies and infections.

Redness inside the ear can be the main sign of infection. If such is the case, then it is highly advised to consult your veterinary doctor in order to prevent any other defect or reaction. Begin the cleaning process of the cat's ears by using ear cleanser or a medicated ear wipe. Such equipment can be easily purchased either from a veterinary doctor clinic or from a pet store. Properly rinse the ear with water after applying the cleanser or the medicated wipe and thoroughly dry it afterwards.

11) Bathing the Turkish Angora cat

Most cats do not tolerate well water bath sessions and show signs of extreme discomfort and anguish. You can avoid a bath if you think that your cat does not take it well. However, just ensure that all the rest of the safety precautions are carefully taken.

You can begin the bathing session by using the special kitty shampoo available at the veterinary shops. Make sure that the shampoo is suitable for your cat by reading the instructions. Do not ever use any shampoo that is meant for dogs or any other animal, as it can cause serious itchy conditions to the cat and can damage the coat of the cat. If necessary, dilute the shampoo with some water. You can also use special cat conditioner, which will give a more healthy and shiny finish to the coat of the cat's body.

Use a washcloth to spread and massage the shampoo throughout the body of the cat.

Avoid shampoo going in the eyes of the cat as it can cause the eyes to itch. Once the massaging is done, then put the cat in a tub filled with water. Just ensure that the head of the cat stays out. Rinse out the shampoo thoroughly by using the shower or using a bath mug all over the body of the cat. After you make sure that all the shampoo is rinsed out, then take a wet cloth and gently rub it all over the cat's body. This will help in removing the loose, dead hairs from the body of the cat.

Then you need to have a dry towel ready. Use it all over the cat's body to thoroughly dry its coat. After this, you are all done with bathing your cat. Hopefully, your Turkish Angora cat would come out very nice, clean and shiny out of the bathroom.

Chapter 11: Feeding the Turkish Angora

1) Nutrition

Nutrition is essential in all cats. Cats such as the Turkish Angora need to obtain important substance, which it will use for energy production or for maintaining the body's metabolic process.

The vet can give you instructions on the important and necessary nutrients that could help your Turkish Angora. The cat may get these nutrients from quality commercial food sold in shops, which are processed to meet various nutritional standards. They contain various nutrients, which are essential for your cat.

These cats are closely related to the fiercest felines like lions and tigers. Turkish Angora cats do not eat everything, it means they are inflexible and as an owner, you must know that. You cannot feed them everything as we do for dogs and other domestic species. Turkish cats do not process an excess of carbohydrates as dogs do and these high carbs damage their digestive system.

An American Association of Feed control has suggested four main types of feed for cats with no exact definition but you may ask your vet to suggest the suitable diet for your Turkish Angora cat.

Firstly, try to feed your cat with a taste test. If it likes to eat one thing, offer it with plenty of feed but try to take some guidelines from an experienced doctor because cats like a little moist and fresh feed.

Normally, a cat needs 200-250 calories per day and this can be completed with one piece of cheese only, however, regarding health issues, you cannot feed your cat with only one feed. As human beings need carbohydrates, protein, and vitamins, cats also need them but in different proportions.

Scientists have researched that different species of cats have different nutrient requirements but if you are more serious about their health, then you must take into account the age, sex, species, and health status of the cat. Kittens need more energy to grow and as they mature, they need less amount of energy to keep them active and healthy.

Vitamins and minerals are also necessary for Turkish Angora cats because they enhance the catalyst reactions and make the cat more attractive, energetic, and smart. Regarding minerals, these should be provided in the diet because animals do not metabolize minerals if they are provided separately. Beet pulp is mostly used in the cat feed because it promotes a healthy gut and avoids undesirable side effects.

Vitamin supplements are not suggested for your Turkish Angora cat because cats do not digest these but you can give them only when a veterinarian diagnoses a mineral deficiency in the cat.

Regarding nutrients, you should consult a nutritionist and can follow nutritional tables provided by the doctors. In case of malnutrition, use a healthy and clean diet for your Turkish Angora cat.

2) Water

To all life, water is very essential to the body system. In the Turkish Angora, the water content comprises about 60 to 70 percent of the total body weight, meaning water plays a major role. The food that the pet takes is either dry foods, which consist of about 10 percent of moisture and also canned food, which has a total percentage of 78% moisture.

This means that for good health, the pet should at least have enough water available in the body. If the pet loses about 10 percent of water, it can lead to serious consequences, which lead to a decrease in weight and other health complications. Water is also essential in the digestive process. The water is used to soften hard foods during the food breakdown in the stomach.

3) Proteins

Proteins are essential. They are the building blocks of cells, tissues, organs, and enzymes. Let us start by discussing what the essential amino acids are. Essential amino acids are the acids in proteins that cannot be broken by the pet in enough quantities. Animal experts insist that such kinds of amino acids must be provided in the diet. These amino acids include:

- Arginine

- Methionine

- Histidine

- Threonine

- Leucine

- Tryptophan

- Taurine

The essential amino acid known as taurine is crucial in the prevention of diseases and helps in reproduction and growth. These kinds of amino acids also help in the sight of the pet. The amino acids can be found easily from eggs, meat and fish.

Non-essential amino acids are important despite their low concentration in amino acids. The proteins obtained from the vegetables can be easily broken down by the pet. The amino acids are found also in cereals and soy. They contain a minimal concentration of glucose, fats and amino acids. They are not found in the diet.

4) Fats

Experts say that fats provide essential energy in bulk. If you wish to provide your pet with the much-needed energy, then fats can provide up to two times more energy than even proteins and carbohydrates. The fats in the body could be used in the production of cells, repairing those that have been wounded and play a major role in the productions of hormones within the body of Turkish Angora.

The fatty acids just like the essential amino acids in proteins can only be given to the pet in the diet. The fats are vital in the absorption of fat-soluble vitamins and the fats protect the inner organs of the pet. The Turkish Angora cannot be given the fats in any other form rather than through diet, this is because the pet will be able to synthesize the fats in the diet. In the breakdown of these fats, water is important.

A slight deficiency in fats could mean skin problems to the pet and a decrease in the total weight of the animal. An acid known as Arachidonic, which is an omega-6 fatty acid, is one of the acids, which plays a great role of maintaining the skin and coat of the Turkish Angora. The acid also plays an important role during reproduction and the kidney functionality of the pet.

Omega-6 and omega -3 fatty acids have an equally essential role in the pet. Both of these fatty acids, which are found in fats, help to heal inflammation. The experts who have experience in the nutrition of the Turkish Angora say that if the omega-6 can be replaced by omega-3, then the fatty acids could help with various parts of the pet. It can help in skin problems, which may be associated with the Turkish Angora, such as allergies.

Arthritis, which is a joint disease, can be rectified using the fatty acids present in fats. Bowel disease can also be healed. An important note here is that if you give the Turkish Angora homemade fats, it will be difficult for you to know or measure the amount of fats you give it.

5) Carbohydrates

Carbohydrates are also energy giving nutrients, which are important to the pet. The carbohydrates are vital and important in the intestinal health of the Turkish Angora. The nutrient is also important in the reproduction process. Diarrhea can be tamed in the small intestine by fibers in carbohydrates that are modified to mix bacterial populace.

For the Turkish Angora to benefit from the fiber found in carbohydrates, they must be in a simpler form for the body to easily absorb them. These fibers must be fermentable. Low fermentable sources lead to poor development and less surface for the intestinal mucosa.

Excess mucus and flatulence is a course of high production of gases and by-products of high fermentable fibers in carbohydrates. Moderate fibers can be easily gotten from beet pulp and they are best known for the promotion of a healthy gut. Other examples of fiber can include corn, wheat and rice.

An important caution is that these fibers are high in energy levels and that is why the experts do not recommend high-energy carbohydrate concentrated foods to younger and growing Turkish Angora. The experts say there is no minimum set amount of carbohydrate requirement for the Turkish Angora; there must be a limitation on the level of glucose that the pet is given.

6) Vitamins

Vitamins are catalysts for enzymes in the pet. The Turkish Angora needs vitamins to catalyze enzymes, keeping in mind the large amount of the vitamins required, they could not be synthesized in the body, hence they are given in the diet. Giving a vitamin supplement is not a wise thing to do on a Turkish Angora; it is deemed unnecessary unless the veterinary expert recommends the supplement vitamin in order to counter a disease or a particular disorder.

Due to more supplement vitamin practice in the recent days, which is commonly known as hypervitaminosis, it has turned to be poisonous. Excess vitamin A may lead to a couple of disorders in the pet. The excess of such a vitamin causes pain in the joints, brittle bones and a dry skin. Excess of vitamin D is not healthy for the Turkish Angora as it may cause bone calcification and pain in the joints. Tiny amounts of vitamins are very essential for the metabolic process in the pet. It is also important to note that vitamins play a key role in catalyzing enzymes that provide the body with energy.

7) Minerals

These nutrients also play a key role in terms of the bodily metabolic process, bone formation, strength and to maintain the fluid balance within the body. Minerals do not give out energy and they are not metabolized at all. The minerals constitute much of the bone structure and they are crucial to the Turkish Angora. In general, minerals are nutrients that the pet's body need for growth and survival. These nutrients cannot be synthesized by the Turkish Angora, hence they are only given in the diet. Cats are very sensitive and you should take care of their diet because like dogs they can't digest everything and odd feeding behaviors alter the whole metabolism.

8) A Word About Milk

Milk can be useful for cats but you need to be extremely careful when using it. The fact is that milk is not healthy for an adult Turkish Angora. Cats are able to tolerate and digest milk only when they are kittens. In adult cats, the digestive system is unable to process dairy products and, therefore, health issues like diarrhea and other digestive issues become quite common.

9) Give your cat a low fat diet

The Turkish Angora is quite an active cat by nature. Unfortunately, if it becomes obese or overweight, you will notice an evident reduction in its activity levels. For an indoor cat, which is not very active, a low fat diet is mandatory.

If you have put your cat on a weight loss diet, you must give him/her adequate amounts of protein. It is true that the calorie intake must be restricted. However, you must always make sure that you do not reduce the amount of essential nutrients. When you increase the amount of proteins, weight loss is aided while keeping the lean body mass intact.

10) Keep a check on the treats

If you are concerned about the health of your cat, make sure you reduce the amount of treats and tidbits. This practice must be extended to at least a couple of weeks after the 'diet' period. You must make sure that everyone in your family is aware of this rule.

If you try and cheat out of affection, remember that you are harming your cat's health. It would help, instead, to cut your cat's meal down to smaller, more frequent meals. This will ensure that he/she does not experience hunger pangs while continuing to stay on a healthy diet.

11) Say no to crash diets

Crash diets are harmful for cats and they are harmful for humans. You must never starve your cat. In fact, no matter what restrictions you make in his/her diet, it must be supervised by a dietician. If you do not keep tabs on the amount of minerals and vitamins your cat is getting, it can lead to a fatal condition called hepatic lipidosis, which affects the liver.

12) Keep the activity levels high

Exercise is extremely important in cats. You cannot control the health and weight of your cat by merely altering the diet. You must ensure that he/she has an active lifestyle. While controlling the calories it takes in, you must also make sure that it burns the calories through exercise and activity. Here are some things you must do to keep make your cat's environment stimulating and engaging:

Set aside a dedicated time to play with your cat. You can use simple toys like strings to help your kitty play and get a good workout.

Allow its natural instincts to take over. You must let your cat climb, scratch and even chase around the house. These exercises are interesting to him/her, by nature, and will increase the process of weight loss.

Get a feeding ball to give your cat for one meal in the day. The advantage with the feeding ball is that your cat will have to put in some amount of effort to roll the ball and get to the food inside.

The food bowl of your cat can be placed on top of a flight of stairs. This will encourage him/her to climb to get to the food.

Try to take your cat outdoors as often as possible. A breath of fresh air will do you and your kitty a great deal of good.

Throughout the process of weight loss, you must be extremely patient. It will take several weeks and even months for your cat to lose weight. If you find it too hard to maintain the weight of your cat on your own, you can ask your vet for tips. You can even enroll in a veterinary weight loss clinic for additional support and information.

Things that are liked by human beings are not always liked by cats. Here we are going to talk about the human graded sushi that is liked by many of us but for cats, it is very dangerous. In raw fish, there is an enzyme called thiamine, which breaks down an essential vitamin "B" in cats. Deficiency of thiamine causes serious neurological conditions in cats.

Onions and chives cause anemia in felines. Don't feed raw onions to your Turkish Angora cat because it will break down red blood cells due to toxic alliums present in onions. Traces of this diet might be used and if they are offered in cooked form then it is a safe diet.

A Turkish Angora cat should not be fed with eggs. We all know that eggs are the best source of protein but uncooked eggs are more prone to salmonella and they might cause a disease called "pancreatitis" in cats. It is an inflammation of the pancreas and leads to severe cases. Eggs can be occasionally fed to cats.

We often feed bones to cats but they are not the right source of energy for them. Bones cause perforation of the intestine and choking in cats. In addition, bones are hard and cat's teeth are not shaped to crush these bones. Hard bones cause teeth fractures in different species of cats.

Although some vets may recommend dry foods for Turkish Angora cats, it is important to note that the health defects caused by kibble are many. It is also possible that the clinic and the curriculum of the veterinary clinic are funded by these pet food companies, making it mandatory for them to recommend dry kibble as a suitable option for your cat's diet. However, the truth is that the nutritional benefits of dry kibble are a lot less than the wet, canned foods.

If you try to save a few hundred dollars on your cat food, remember that you will end up paying several hundred dollars in helping your cat recover from nutrition related issues. Remember that your cat food must be a good source of protein. If you are unable to do that, he/she will be malnourished and unhealthy.

Cheaper varieties of cat food will only be able to provide your cat with plant based proteins. For an animal that is an obligate carnivore, the only good source of protein is animal protein. In addition to this, these cheap foods also contain high amounts of carbohydrates that can make your cat obese or diabetic. Make sure you only bring home high quality foods for your pet.

According to the requirements, your Turkish Angora cat needs only 200-250 calories a day. You can offer cheese but in very little amounts. Try not to feed your cat a human diet because it causes digestive problems and human vitamin supplements damage the inner lining of the feline's digestive tract. The kidneys and liver are also damaged by feeding your cat a human dietary supplement.

Try to contact a veterinarian urgently in case of food poisoning because cats are very sensitive and can't bear serious health problems. If you are consulting feeding charts and feed them a specialized diet then you are the lucky one to have a healthy, smart, and active cat.

13) Foods you must never give your cat

The kinds of foods that your cat eats and you eat are extremely different from each other. The entire digestive ability is quite different and hence, the food should also be significantly different.

Many pet owners make the mistake of giving their cats the same food that is cooked in their home. Now, let's put it this way, do you think of dry kibble or canned fish as an appropriate food for you? Well, then how do you expect your cat to fulfill its nutritional requirements with the foods that you eat?

Usually pet owners think that their little beauties are sure of what is best for them. Cats are known to be picky eaters but there is little evidence that suggests that a cat knows what is right for it and what is wrong. Perhaps in the wild, cats follow their instincts and get the right nutrition. However, with domesticated cats, the varieties of foods that are available to them will make them reach out for all the wrong goodies.

Not only are these foods nutritionally poor, they can also be quite dangerous for your Turkish Angora. As we mentioned earlier, it is very easy to feed your cat the wrong things. They will enjoy just about anything that you feed them. In addition, in the assumption that your cat is happy, you will continue to give him/her food that can causes serious health related issues. Here are some foods that are a complete no-no for your beloved pet:

Tuna

Although this does sound strange, there is a good chance that your cat will get addicted to tuna. Of course a share of tuna now and then should not harm your cat too much. However, a steady tuna diet can cause malnutrition in your cat. Although cats savor tuna and really enjoy it, the nutrients available are not too many. Another common issue with tuna is mercury poisoning. Never keep open tuna cans within the reach of your cat. You can serve it occasionally but make sure that he knows that it is not available all the time.

Chives, Garlic, Onion

These are common ingredients in all our foods but they have disastrous health impacts on cats. Any form of these vegetables, cooked, powdered or even raw can cause anemia in cats by completely breaking down their red blood cells. Even though human baby food consists of powdered onion, do not consider it safe for your kitty. Onion poisoning and even gastrointestinal problems might arise if your cat eats chives, garlic or onion.

Alcohol

Your cat must never ever consume any form of alcohol. Make sure that all the liquor in your home is out of your cat's reach. The effects on the cats' liver and brain are similar to the effects on the human brain. In cats, however, the amount of alcohol required to do this damage is a lot lesser. A 5 pound cat can go into a coma with just two teaspoons of liquor. Even one teaspoon more can be fatal for your kitty.

Raisins and Grapes

Many cat owners consider grapes and raisins as suitable treats for their cats. This is never a good idea. Giving your cat too many raisins or grapes can also lead to kidney failure eventually. Even a small share of grapes can really make your cat fall sick. Vomiting is one early sign of illness caused by grapes. Some cats may have no reactions but we are not sure of the long-term effects of feeding grapes to your cat.

Caffeine
An overdose of caffeine can actually kill your cat. With caffeine intake, there is no antidote either. The most common symptoms of caffeine poisoning in cats include restlessness, fast-paced breathing, heart palpitations and muscle tremors.

Caffeine is not only found in coffee. There are several other sources including beans, chocolates, colas and even energy drinks like red bull. Some medicines and painkillers also contain substantial amounts of caffeine.

Chocolate
It is impossible to say no to your adorable cat staring at you while you gorge on chocolate. However, this treat can end up being extremely harmful for your little pet. Chocolate consists of a toxic material known as theobromine. This is extremely dangerous for cats. It is found in all forms of chocolate including white chocolate. The common problems associated with chocolate are muscle tremors, seizures, heart changes and even death.

Candy
Any sweetened food including candy, gum, toothpaste and baked goods contain an element called xylitol. This element can pace up the circulation of insulin in the cat's body. As a result, the level of sugar in the cat's body drops suddenly, causing seizures and liver failure in your cat.

Bones and Fat Trimmings
Scraps from the table are fed so often to cats but they may cause serious health disorders in cats. Fat, whether cooked or uncooked, can result in vomiting, diarrhea and intestinal problems in your

cat. If a cat chokes on a bone, it can be fatal. Other problems related to the bones are lacerations and obstructions due to the splinters.

Raw Eggs

Many people believe that raw eggs are a healthy dietary option for their cat. However, this is not true. There are two primary health issues that result from consumption of raw eggs. Firstly, food poisoning may occur due to the presence of bacteria like E coli. Secondly, a certain protein in the egg white, known as avidin, can reduce the absorption of vitamin B in cats leading to skin related issues.

Raw Meat

Although many of you may argue that cats only eat raw meats in the wild, the truth is that uncooked meat and fish can be harmful to cats. They contain bacteria and microorganisms that might cause food poisoning. Additionally, certain enzymes present in raw fish can destroy essential vitamins like thiamine in the cat's body. This can cause neurological problems and can also result in a coma in extreme cases.

Dog Food

A bite once in a while will not harm your cat too much. However, the formula used in dog food is definitely not suitable for cats. Cat food is packed with necessary proteins and vitamins that can help the cat fulfill its nutritional requirements. On the other hand, dog foods can also contain plant proteins that are not suitable for your cat. If your cat regularly consumes dog food, it might become malnourished.

Liver

Giving your cat liver once in a while is not an issue. However, too much consumption of liver can lead to vitamin A toxicity in cats. This is a serious condition as it affects the bones. There might be deformities and also bone growths and spurts on the spine.

Osteoporosis can also be observed in cats with vitamin A toxicity. In extreme cases it can be fatal.

Yeast Dough
Uncooked dough is never recommended for a cat. If it is consumed by the cat, there are chances that the dough will actually raise inside the cat's stomach. During this expansion, the dough may stretch the abdomen in the cat and also cause alcohol poisoning as the yeast ferments.

Many times, being cautious isn't good enough. Your cat might just make its way into your pantry and have a generous helping of restricted foods. There is no need to be alarmed. In most cases, your vet will be able to provide an antidote to take care of the situation for you.

Chapter 12: Traveling with your Turkish Angora

Sadly, cats are not the best travel companions. If you have had a dog for a pet, never assume that your Turkish Angora will be as easy to travel with. Cats are extremely fussy travelers and you must take utmost care to ensure that they do not feel too distressed when you are taking them out for a considerably long ride.

1) Traveling in a car

Remember that you must never leave the cat open in the car. If your cat decides to pounce on the driver, the repercussions could be fatal. Make sure that you always carry your cat in a carrier. The carrier should be extremely sturdy and must be made from metallic wires or even fiber glass. The carriers made from light plastic or even cardboard are not meant for long journeys. They are only suitable for short trips like a visit to the vet.

The weather that you travel in is extremely important in deciding what measures you need to take while traveling, if you think that it will get hotter as you proceed, make sure that you get a carrier that allows a good amount of air circulation. In case it is going to get cold along the way, carry enough blankets to wrap your cat up and keep him warm.

There are also draft free carriers that will ensure that you do not leave your kitty shivering and uncomfortable. Irrespective of the kind of carrier that you buy, there is one more thing that you need to consider. In case you are planning to change your mode of transport along the way, plane for example, you must also check for the guidelines that they provide with respect to the type of carrier that is allowed.

If you have ample space in the back of your car and you only intend to travel by car, you can even use a large crate to keep your cat in. All you need to do is place blankets and sheets inside this crate and put it in the back of your car. The only thing that you need to ensure is that you provide your cat with a quiet place where he/she can rest during the journey. Place his/her favorite toys and treats around him/her to reduce the stress of traveling. The bedding that you provide during the traveling period should be one that he/she is already used to.

Make sure that the crate or the carrier is completely secure. Even if you were to apply the brakes suddenly, it must be safe. If the carrier or crate falls suddenly, your cat will be startled. The last thing you want while traveling is an anxious cat. If you are driving in a hatchback, never allow the cat to be placed in the boot as this area is very dark and badly ventilated. Check on your cat regularly and make sure that he/she is comfortable.

2) Traveling by train

When you are traveling by train, you must obviously place your cat in a carrier. Since there are several other strangers on a train, you do not want to have any instances of your cat breaking free and scaring them.

So, make sure that the carrier that you have is extremely sturdy. The base of the carrier must be extremely strong to ensure that your cat is secured. The carrier must be light so that you do not have any difficulty carrying it around. It must also be of a convenient size depending upon the space available on the train. Make sure that you get a carrier that is large enough for your cat to rest in. Never cram your kitty into a small carrier because there isn't enough storage space.
You must keep a familiar blanket in the carrier to reduce anxiety. However, littering and soiling can be quite a concern. So, line

your cat's cage with a good amount of absorbent paper so that you may both have a pleasant journey.

3) Traveling by air

Traveling with your pet by air requires a good deal of planning in advance. The airlines that you choose will also depend upon their efficiency in handling and transferring your cat. Most airlines will not allow the carrier into the cabin area. You may have to let your pet travel alone in a special section on the aircraft that is reserved for pets.

Cats will have very little trouble traveling by air. If you have a pregnant cat or a kitten less than three months of age traveling with you, it might become a matter of concern. It is recommended that you avoid air travel for these two categories of cats.

Check for a license to transport animals in the airlines that you choose. Chances are that you and your cat will travel by separate flights. If this is true, make sure that you get a direct flight for your cat so that he/she does not have to deal with issues like transits and transfers.

Traveling with your Turkish Angora can be fun if you prepare him/her in advance. The most important thing to do is to condition it to enjoy sitting inside the carrier. If you are able to accomplish this, you have already won half the battle.

Chapter 13: Caring for the Turkish Angora

Health is a very important aspect of the Turkish Angora's life. Though once in a while along the way, illness is inevitable, something of the utmost importance is how you deal with it. Cats such as the Turkish Angora are no exemptions since they are animals too and just like our everyday pals, or kids, they have to be cared for to remain healthy.

Simple yet complicated like any other animal care, this cat's health is equally wide and ranges from averting simple illnesses to just be fine and maintaining its fitness. A well cared for cat is therefore a role model of how cheap, and easy, living with a cat can be.

1) Signs and symptoms of illness

Come to think of it, doesn't care for that Turkish Angora cat just give you joy when you see it purring and bouncing around with mirth all day long? Of course it does, however you must have a very keen eye for health and a perfect relationship with your cat to be able to tell whether it's healthy, ill, or just pulling your leg for a little groom. As the primary care giver to the cat, you should understand that it's your core duty to pay attention to your cat and always be there for it.

If illness knocks however, you should be aware that different pets will exhibit sickness symptoms differently and so shall the Turkish Angora cat. These signs and symptoms will vary in greater lengths but will still be evidently vivid if you pay the Angora close attention. Therefore, knowledge of these symptoms will prove very important since it will help you to even get to your vet on time in any case sickness strikes. With a robust ability to notice any slight change, the cat's sickness will never get you off guard.

a. Strange Behavior

Your cat will rarely show signs of any strange behavior unless something is wrong. When the strong and fond Angora starts to display simple, questionable behavior, it might just be a sign of an imminent illness disaster and therefore care has to be taken. You should therefore start keeping it in sight.

Behaviors such as frequent visits to the litter box will be a very open factor to raise eyebrows. While most cats will tend to visit their litter boxes twice a day, some might just do so as often as the meals come in.

Yet in cases where your cat goes to urinate or defecate more that its normal rate, be weary that you might be on your way to the vet pretty soon. It is therefore prudent to always take a closer peep to your cat's litter box before you change or clean it to see if you can spot anything strange in it like traces of blood in the urine. This is because with such visible signs it is easy to tell if the cat is sick or not.

However, such behavior as acute loss of appetite are not signs to be brushed off so easily. If your cat stops to run after it's eating bowl, or just smells its favorite meal and walks away, and has not eaten in a whole day, something must be really wrong.

You should keep close tabs on your cat for at least 24hrs, you never know, there might just have been a cat party at the neighbor's yard. Cats at times also lose their mind due to mental disorders; although this might be hard to determine, be mindful of head tilting, dizziness, or disorientation. All these might be definite signs of neurological disorder, so in such cases, always be quick to do the right thing and visit the vet.

As we have seen before, a cat's personality is well defined. Unique only to every cat, it is no doubt its own way of telling who it is. Cats love to play, to exercise, and to run around all day long, but if lately your cat exhibits an exquisite form of tiredness, or exhaustion chances are its suffering from some deficiency syndromes. For example, lethargy and apathy are very great symptoms of vitamin deficiency in these lovely creatures as previously seen.

Did you know that Angoras love to swim? This does not mean that they should be frequently found in the bathtubs or playing "hide and seek" in the kitchen sinks. Such constant behavior might just manifest the cat's frustration at something.

It might be trying to grab your attention for the wrong reasons. So maybe it's time to find out what's really bothering it, maybe walk it back to the vet, or just push it across its weighing scale. This way you may just be sure to note one or two abnormalities, since factors such as constant weight loss are just direct pointers to deteriorating health.

You must understand that your cat also has mood swings and emotions that can go out of control. If you have observed a sudden change in the behavior of your Turkish Angora, it can be linked to emotional stress.

b. Symptoms of Stress

With a well behaved cat like the Turkish Angora, it is very easy to notice the symptoms of stress. The most common symptoms include:

- Loss of appetite

- Reduced interaction with the members in the family

- Aggressive behavior

- Confinement to hiding places

- Elimination out of the litter box

- Too much grooming

- Change in interaction with other pets in the house

It is possible that your cat displays more symptoms of stress, including a change in voice. It is impossible to compare the symptoms seen in two different cats. The intensity of the symptoms varies from one cat to another.

While in some cats, the change is very drastic, some of them show such gradual progression that it is very easy to ignore. The Turkish Angora cat loves to interact. So, you must always be alert to behavior patterns like excessive hiding to make sure that you do not allow the emotional distress in your cat to escalate.

2) What Causes Stress in Turkish Angora Cats?

There are several causes for stress in cats. Now, there are some factors that we do not even consider potent enough to cause dramatic changes in the cat's behavior. However, there are many changes in the immediate environment of the cat that seem too ordinary for us. However, the impact that it has on your pet can be extremely damaging. These normal and usually overlooked causal factors include:

- Installation of new carpets

- Loud Music

- Change in the brand of litter

- Dirty litter box

- Inclusion of new furniture

- Visitors

- Repairs in the house

- Barking of dogs

- Appearance of strange cats or dogs around the house

- Travel

- Change in the brand of food

Then, there are some causal factors that are very evident, as they have emotionally damaging effects on human beings as well. These factors include:

- Divorce

- Death in the Family

- Birth of baby

- Illness in the Family

- Abuse

- Inclusion of another pet

- Natural disasters

- Injuries

- Moving to a new home

Cats, as we have discussed in previous Chapters, need to get used to the sights and smells around them in order to be comfortable. However, if you make sudden changes in your cat's environment, you can expect it to feel distressed. It is possible that over time, your cat will overcome these issues. If they persist, however, it is a good idea to consult an animal therapist. Even your regular veterinary doctor will be able to check your cat for emotional distress and provide you with necessary solutions.

3) How to Reduce Emotional Stress in Turkish Angoras

When you see one or more of the signs mentioned above, the first thing you need to do is have your Turkish Angora cat examined by a doctor. The reason for stress must be identified at the earliest. Although this is not easy, you can do a background check to come to suitable conclusions. The triggers for stress in your Turkish Angora are not always evident. However, if you are aware of the sensitivity level in your cat, you will be able to determine the most obvious causes for stress.

It is important for you to understand that the hearing and smelling abilities of your feline companion are far better than yours. Even the faintest sound or smell that is easily neglected by you is picked up by your cat quite easily. Scents from another cat, new smells inside the house like fresh paint, scents of new people etc. can be very stressful for your cat. So, if you are aware of any changes that have taken place around your cat's environment, you must include it in the list of suspected causes.

Here are some things that you can do to reduce stress in your cat:

Prepare your cat for any big change that is impending.

Have enough spaces in the house where your cat can rest or hide. If your cat does not want to be bothered, allow it to have a safe retreat.

The litter box must be kept pristine. Try to keep the entire set up appealing to your cat. The location of the litter box, the type of litter used and the number of boxes you include should be given a good amount of thought.

If there are several cats in your house and you notice tension and change in behavior amongst them, you need to make several modifications. You must make sure that every cat in your home feels completely secure in its environment.

If your cat is getting too much attention from kids and visitors, keep it away from them. Even if the other pets in your home are giving it unnecessary attention, you should provide your cat with a space where it will be able to spend some time alone, in peace.

Make sure you spend enough time with your cat. You must engage in interactive sessions and play with your cat to give it confidence. This is the only way you can develop a positive relationship with your cat based on affection and trust.

Cats never appreciate change. So, try to make them minimal, especially with things that are associated with the cat directly, like food, litter box and even water bowl. Any change around your cat must be gradual to help it accommodate it.

Enrich your cat's environment. Turkish Angoras get bored very easily and must be constantly engaged. So, try to include toys, puzzles and even entertainment DVDs as part of your stimulation kit. You must always ensure that your cat is having fun.

Never leave the cat alone. If you are traveling, get someone to take care of your cat. Turkish Angora cats especially get extremely distressed when they are away from their owners even for one day.

The interactions that you have with your cat are extremely important in its emotional well being. If you do notice stress in your cat, there is no need to be alarmed. All you have to do is give him/her as much time and affection as you can to help it get back to his/her old, playful self.

In all, never try to diagnose your cat. Though you may be its immediate friend, it is important to humbly recognize cat diagnosis as being far from your expertise. Just understand your cat and come to appreciate observation as the key to this bond. Most of all understand that a well fed, rested, and protected cat is likely to remain healthier for longer.

a. Physical Clues
Physical clues are another greater than life factor to consider. Generally, a physical outlook would be quite revealing to any source of pain or illness that a person or an animal might be going through.

Discharge usually is the most conspicuous of the physical consideration. From excessive mucus in the nose, teary eyes, to bloody, or shaggy fur, it would be very easy to tell if your cat is unwell. However, frequent grooming of your cat may just as well give you an edge to easily detect these physical injuries and pain. Usually seen on the outer coat of your cat or by simply grooming your cat's fur, physical clues should still reveal volumes up to the well hidden kidney stones disorders.

Cats love to be touched and touching is a universal way of sensing, no more than hearing or tasting. It is therefore advisable to constantly groom your cat for lumps. Being swellings on the cat's skin or body, lumps will often be noticed only by touching.

That is why touching would be a more viable way to do it. Just like their human counterparts, female cats for instance are prone to breast cancer and grooming would be the perfect way to find out if this underlying threat might be knocking at your favorite pet.

Some sicknesses however will allow your eyes to do a fantastic job for you. A sickness that causes the cat's pupils to be dilated falls squarely in this category. If your cat's eyes are dilated or if one pupil is more dilated than the other, it is no doubt that your cat should see its vet. In addition to this, respiratory problems will manifest themselves vividly if you are always in constant contact with your cat.

This works well with a combination of many other factors. For instance you walk into your apartment, and suddenly your cat that jumps on your lap has this whizzing sound in its breathing. What suddenly crosses your mind? A difficulty in breathing most definitely and the opposite is also true, when your cat breathes very fast, heavily, or weakly, something must be going a miss, so don't hesitate to pick up your phone and dial that number that you know best, the vet's.

Again that is not enough, usually traits of sicknesses may run over and over again, but even in that recurrence those few that may stand out or generalize the rest, like discoloration of the cat's gums and unkempt coat are the main factors that adds strength to these content of physique. Black or very pale gums, together with paleness around the eyes and ears would specifically point to an ill cat.

Though a foul smell from the mouth might indicate the same, nothing is more crystal clear than unkempt fur or the loss of so much fur on the coat. The latter may depict stress due to change of environment or simply sickness and an urgent need to see a vet.

Sometimes your cat may act strangely with mucus, blood, and a discolored coat and this must be checked out. Consultation is the best medicine for these many diseases.

4) Examining for specific illnesses

Questions of whether your cat is going to be fine, or if it will make it through might just stress your mind, but with a rough idea, you can always calmly take it to the vet with no hesitation of an end of the odds. With a little help you can always be able to relate your cat's symptoms with more specific illnesses and this way you are able to know what urgent measures to take.

You know life has a way of getting back at us when we really hoped for the best. Here are some specific illnesses:

a. Fleas Infestation

Fleas are a very common source of infections to many domesticated animals, even that Turkish Angora that you are so fond of is not immune to them. Therefore, if you see your cat scratching often do an immediate spot check, by running a fine tooth comb through the coat while maintaining an eye for those tiny little black insects.

You can also lie them down on a sheet of white paper and see if any will fall off; if that is the case, ask your vet for the right medication. Fleas in most cases may act as a source of discomfort to your cat, and as if to add salt to the wound, they will make your kittens anemic, or worse transmit other infections such as *Ctenocephalides Felis* commonly known as the cat flea and which always carry worms with it.

b. Hairballs
Formed at the back of the throat or in the small intestines, hairballs will cause a bad smell in your cat's mouth. In extreme cases hairballs may become matted hair or cause undigested foul-smelling food as feces or vomit, leading to an eventual surgery of your cat.

To solve this, ensure that you groom your cat often and give the cat a balanced diet to allow it to pass out the hairballs or just cough it out. Pumpkin pulp would add fiber to digest down the hair ball and egg yolk would do just great in adding proteins that break down the hairball, therefore you may just consider adding these to your cat recipe and serving it with a balanced diet.

c. Overactive Thyroid and Constipation
Characterized by increased appetite, thirst or unexplained weight loss, an overactive thyroid will be a great source of weakness, nervousness, vomiting, lethargy, diarrhea, and messy coat. The best way to deal with is to see your vet and ensure the right medication for your cat.

With dry, hard stool, it is easy to tell if your cat is constipated. Cats get constipated due to very many reasons, such as ingestion of foreign objects, enlarged prostate gland, dehydration, low fiber diet, or maybe the effects of specific medications. While the signs are so broad and confusion imminent, getting the right advice or medication is the best way to ensure that your Turkish Angora is safe.

d. Feline Diabetes
Also known as diabetes mellitus, this is common in almost all cat breeds. Feline diabetes includes increased urination (polyuria) vomiting, dehydration, weakness, loss of appetite, and increased

thirst (polydipsia). Breathing abnormalities and in most cases an unkempt coat will also accompany its symptoms and signs.

Though it may affect cats of all ages, it is more common with older cats 10 years old and above or obese male cats. The best way to find out is to take your cat for blood and urine sugar sampling as this will assure you of a concrete medication and dependable results.

5) Medical Disorders

From the topic "examining for specific illnesses" we see how you can use different signs to find out if your Turkish Angora is ill or not and even add a few pointers to what they might be suffering from.

However, it doesn't show us what exactly they may be suffering from since medical disorders are so many, and while you are very much advised against diagnosing your own cat, it is of great advantage to know what the vet will be treating your cat for, and better still, it will feel easier if you just had a little knowledge prior to your meeting with the vet. This way you will be sure to ask relevant questions or even to have a better idea of the understanding what is required of you.

a. Feline Immunodeficiency Virus (FIV)
Belonging to the same group as Human Immunodeficiency Virus, this medical disorder belongs purely to cats. FIV with its slow viruses is known for its lifelong infections and slow progressive diseases.

b. Feline Leukemia Virus (FeLV)
This is a feline retrovirus that causes both cancerous and non cancerous diseases. It is easily destroyed by detergents, warmth, and will not survive long outside your cat. Carried mostly in urine, tears, and feces of infected cats, it is not contagious, but only by a direct, prolonged, wet contact with the infected cats.

There is no evidence that FeLV would be transmittable to humans.

c. Cat Ringworm
The most common of all skin infections in domestic cats is a fungal infection spread through spores. This disorder may not bother your cat, since it is a self limiting disease and will come and go as it pleases, however treating it might also be difficult and the scars might be difficult to remove.

d. Feline Infectious Peritonitis (FIP)
The leading cause of cat deaths, the most feared disease of the domesticated cats, FIP has wiped out many cats. Caused by a corona virus infection, FIP has proven hard to diagnose as most of its tests are never accurate. It is for this reason too that it has managed to lead to the deaths of many cats.

e. Feline Urinary Tract Disease
This is always a combination of different symptoms and may just be readily confused with other diseases. Diseases of the urinary tract occur mostly in cats affecting both males and females in greater numbers. They affect the bladder through the urethra. Sometimes it may lead to the obstruction of the urinary tract system and to eventual death. However, it has a better diagnosis, better symptoms, and so it's readily understood and well treated so don't be worried

There are also other age related disorders that you should be aware of, just like human beings, as the cats grow older, so does their immunity. At this stage they are more vulnerable and prone to opportunistic diseases. Considering age as an immediate factor will also allow you to understand the frequent medical disorders that your cat faces. So in as much as you want to consider your cat stronger, be cautious and think twice upon its age.

6) Spaying and Neutering

Controlled animal breeding is very essential. Different people have different tastes for different animal sexes. While some would prefer male pets, others would love to be associated with the female. All these may just emanate from the fact that both male and female breeds of animals are portrayed to possess different characteristics.

The male is considered at times brutal and masculine, while the female, subtle. Cats are not unfamiliar to this "animal prejudice." Whatever sex of the Turkish Angora you choose you should understand that control of your animal "heat" and eventual breeding should be a thought worth pondering.

Spaying and neutering are special procedures carried out by prominent veterinarians to ensure that the cat is incapable of reproducing by removing the necessary organs. In the female cats, the fallopian tube, the uterus and the ovaries are removed while in the male, castration and removal of testicles is practiced. In females this process is known as spaying while in the males it is known as neutering.

We have had quite a rising number of abandoned cats being taken in by animal control systems. You may also want to maintain only a specific number of cats as pets. Irrespective of the number you choose, you will not desire whatsoever to find your cat roaming further from home or you may not desire to find a spontaneous rise in their numbers overnight.

A healthy, well taken care of pet is an image you may wish to gallantly sell across the streets. Who doesn't love to be associated with success in any field anyway? This is the more reason why spaying and neutering simply comes in handy in control of the cat's breeding.

Feline overpopulation is a common problem these days. Even with a predominantly indoor cat like the Turkish Angora, there are chances that the cat will mate with other strays. This may lead to kittens either in your home or in the streets. This is a problem either way as feline overpopulation has very painful and sad consequences.

It is true that several shelters are euthanizing cats to make room for homeless kittens and also kittens that have been rescued.

If every cat owner takes the responsibility of neutering and spaying seriously, these unpleasant conditions can be controlled to a large extent.

a. How to Spay or Neuter

Like any other domesticated animal of its kind, a spaying operation involves the administration of general anesthetic and the surgical removal of the ovaries from the uterus through an incision made at the belly of the cat. Usually, the vet will ask you to withhold food for at least 12 hours prior to the surgery in order to minimize potential anesthetic complications.

For the castration of the male, the incisions are made on the scrotum to remove the ovaries, and the food doesn't necessarily have to be withheld. The cats will usually recover from this neutering process very quickly, come the following day after surgery, they should be up and well again, but if yours is unusually quiet, please show concern and inform your vet immediately.

b. When to Spay or Neuter

If you intend to spay your cat or to neuter it, you should do it before it gets a litter or even its first heat. The process of spaying or neutering is best done before the cat reaches puberty. You should also note that your cat can be spayed as a kitten but not before it reaches at least 8 weeks or if it weighs less than two pounds. In fact in America, the American Veterinary Medical Association supports early spaying and neutering as the best period possible for any of the two to be carried out. Completely armed with this knowledge, you will appreciate the subsequent reasons for spaying and neutering.

120

In case you have neglected spaying or neutering, you can even take your cat to the vet when he or she is in heat. However, with female cats, spaying when they are in heat will lead to excessive blood loss. If you think that you want your adult cat to be neutered or spayed, you can consult your vet about the safety of the procedure.

c. Improved Quality

If you are a person who only wants to have a cat as a pet, you may just find this reason really fulfilling. See, humanity has been modifying domesticated animals to better suit their human needs for centuries. With controlled propagation of selected animal breeds to improve quality, man has achieved greater milestones in successful animal breeding. Just like culling that deals with sorting out animals bred by removing the smaller and weaker animals and concentrates on breeding the much better quality, spaying and neutering does the same only in a different way, through making your cat barren or impotent.

This in turn will help your cat to harness energy. You see, cats are very agile and playful pets. As a completely active cat, the male may become wild by wandering away from home in pursuit of the female, to quench its desire to mate. The female on the other hand will be having kittens after every successful gestation. In both cases, the cats use a lot of energy and this makes their health rapidly deteriorate, leaving you with an emaciated cat for a pet.

However, when they are neutered, the cat's needs are limited and it grows stronger, bigger and healthier. In fact, even its life span is improved, movement controlled and therefore it's not vulnerable to diseases.

No matter what surgical procedure your cat is going to undergo, a good amount of preparation is mandatory. You can get all the necessary pre-surgical advice from your vet. Make sure you adhere to all the guidelines. The most common precaution to take is to ensure that your cat does not eat anything after midnight until the surgery.

If you are taking a kitten for operation, on the other hand, the nutritional requirements are drastically different. Following these measures will ensure that there are no complications during the surgery and after.

d. Controlled Breeding

Cats can also be kept for breeding purposes. If you are choosing a cat for this very reason, you may want to go for the best. Yet again it's not every single day that you will want your cat to breed, if you are not doing so for commercial purposes, or even if you were, there will reach a point that you will consider the number of cats in your yard to be enough. Or so it will come to pass that you will want to control a lesser breed and maintain the better one or that you will consider your cat's age to be less ideal if conceived.

These reasons will allow you to look for a controlled system of breeding, and spaying just provides the remedy. Either way, as a cat owner you will only get to achieve either your ideal number of cats, or your ideal type of breed, meticulous, right?

e. Reduced Hostility

No one likes a hostile pet. Everyone likes his or her pet-cat to be subtle, warm, welcoming, and very easy to relate to. While this is the case it is not the reality, you will find most cats that have not been spayed quite hostile and very much hot blooded. This reason is attributed to their desire for the opposite sex.

Neutering will therefore be a very viable way to reduce your cat's hostility. This prevents your cat from exposing itself to dangerous situations such as cat fights over a mating partner. Your cat will therefore become friendlier to you and to your loved ones. In fact by the end of this process, you can enjoy the comfort of your home, knowing that even your children are safe from the constant cat claws.

There is no apparent change in the cat's personality after neutering or spaying. It is true that the cat might be quiet and calm and not too playful for a while but he or she will get back to its original self as soon as it recovers.

There are several myths that a Turkish Angora cat will become lethargic or obese after neutering or spaying. This prevents most people from considering this rather important procedure.

You may have to provide your cat with a certain diet after neutering or spaying. This is to ensure that the cat gets all the nutrients and calories required during the recovery process. If you have any concerns about the process of neutering or spaying, your vet will be able to provide you with all possible details.

f. Reduced Infections
Usually cats experience even their first heat much earlier than anticipated. If you take the advantage and neuter your cat early, it will save it from cancerous diseases, that can either be transmitted by other cats to it or other infections that may be acquired due to lack of hygiene.

7) Vaccinations

There are core vaccines that every cat must have and then there are some that are for specific breeds, called non-core vaccines.

Panleukopenia should be given strictly between 6 to 8 weeks. This one will be given to your cat before it is taken in by you. It puts off the fear of the cat being exposed to the other at home that may make it fall sick or infect it in any possible way before it adapts to its new environment.

After being administered that very first time, the vaccine is to be administered again after every 3 to 4 weeks until the kitten gets to week 16. This very first vaccine is always combined with feline viral respiratory disease complex vaccines in one dose.

1 or 2 years later, cats who love to mix with other cats are given a booster that will boost their immunity. The Turkish Angora should also be taken care of in this manner. In fact, it is suggested that it

should have all the three sets of vaccines since it is the most outgoing and affectionate of all cat breeds.

Vaccinations are important for all animals, especially home pets, and have immense benefits that will help you recognize what a beautiful cat you have for a pet. Even though it is specifically intended for the cat, you will find that cat a vaccination usually has greater underlying benefits for you too, if not also for your household. Therefore much attention should be paid while doing it and ensure that while doing it, you strictly adhere to its timetable.

a. Fighting Infections
As a cat lover, you must have guessed that such benefits would come with vaccination. Vaccines help your cat in boosting its immune system, helping your cat to fight infections; it ensures that the disease causing micro organisms become obsolete. Within most of these vaccines are dead microorganisms that when administered into your cat's immune system produces proteins called antibodies, so that when your cat encounters the actual living microorganisms those antibodies "fights" the infection.

These antibodies will therefore have your cats back. Kittens are even more vulnerable to these diseases since their immune systems are not totally developed and their only remedy is the vaccination. Though they still get some antibodies from their already vaccinated mothers through the breast milk, vaccination proves that it still wheels around the chain of the cat's lives and health.

b. Preservation of Breeds
The precious furry and most assertive cat breed of all, the Turkish Angora almost phased out in the 1900 and was been saved by the controlled programs that have been set up in Turkey. The success of such programs can only be attributed to the supportive side of a well structured vaccination program. This has ensured that this breed that most of us love so has beautifully weathered the storm of time.

8) After Vaccination, What's Next?

Typically, cats, just like humans, may experience side effects when antibodies are introduced to their system. These side effects usually vary and should be no cause for alarm as they always knock them off. However, if they become persistent, a vet's advice must be rapidly sought.

The side effects can develop within hours of vaccination. Milder side effects may include swelling and discomfort at the vaccination site, lethargy, or decreased appetite. However, the more serious symptoms that occur less often would be persistent vomiting, diarrhea, severe breathing difficulties, or eventual collapse.

These require you to always put your doctor on alert, as they can be life threatening or suddenly just turn to instant emergencies. With the swelling of vaccination areas, this may last for up to weeks later. If it doesn't disappear in two weeks, seek medical attention.

In rare cases, your cat might need an operation. Your cat might experience a little discomfort after these processes. These procedures very seldom have a painful recovery process. If it is in pain, you must make sure you either leave it under specialized care or consult your vet regularly. There are a few precautions that you can take to ensure that the recovery process is comfortable and safe.

Give your cat a safe place in the house to rest during the recovery process. This place should not be accessible by other pets or even children.

Do not encourage jumping or running during this recovery process. You can take it out on walks but make sure that he/she is not physically exerted.

The area that has been operated upon should not be licked. So, getting your cat an Elizabethan collar is the best option.

During the recovery process, avoid using litter in the litter box. Instead, use shredded paper. The problem with sand or litter is that the dust can cause unwanted infections.

The site with the incision must be cleaned regularly to avoid infections.

You must always look out for symptoms like:

- Redness in the site of incision

- Swelling in the site of incision

- Discharge from the area

- Reduced appetite

- Vomiting

- Lethargy

If you do notice one or more symptoms, inform your vet to improve the recovery process.

Chapter 14 : Finding a Good Vet

You will find a lot of Turkish Angora Cat 101 online. In any case, it is necessary for you to have a reliable vet who you can trust with your pet. It is never a good idea to constantly change the vet who treats your Turkish Angora. Cats, as you know, do not appreciate change. They are usually reluctant to cooperate with vets.

You must give your cat time to get accustomed to the touch and voice of one vet. Once he/she is comfortable with him or her, your cat will be more relaxed during vet visits. A vet is an important part of your cat's life and you must make sure you look for the perfect one to take care of your pet.

There will be several large and small veterinary clinics around your town. So, it can be quite confusing when you set out to choose something for your precious pet. The best way to look for a vet is to ask for recommendations from your friends and neighbors. If you know people in the neighborhood who have had pets for a long time, they will be able to recommend someone to you.

You must make a conscious effort to look for someone who is specialized in cat care. The section of veterinary care is growing rapidly and you will definitely find someone in the vicinity.

In order to be prepared for an emergency, here are some things that you might want to consider before you zero in on one vet:

- How far is your vet from your home?

- Is the commuting time too long?

- In case of an emergency, will you make it on time to the vet?

127

- Is the ambiance of the clinic feasible for your cat?

It is always better to find someone close to your house. It must not take more than 15 minutes to drive down to your vet. Even if it is not an emergency, remember that your cat is not particularly fond of long drives.

Once you have found someone who seems to fit into all the requirements, you can make a trial visit. The chemistry between your cat and the vet is extremely important if you want to make it a long lasting relationship.

There are some signs that will indicate how comfortable you and your pet will be in a particular clinic. Make the following observations if you are visiting for the first time:

The waiting room must be well maintained.

The ambience must be comforting for the cat so that it feels secure when being examined.

If it is a common clinic for dogs and cats, how are they maintained when they are admitted for hospital care? Are they kept in separate cages?

The people at the reception must be friendly. These people are going to be your point of contact in the coming sessions and you must be comfortable with them.

Once you are in the examination room, check how the vet interacts with pets and their owners. The tone must be soothing. It must be able to provide undivided attention to your cat. The vet must value your opinions about your cat's health and must be respectful towards you.

The personality of your vet plays an important role in the way it interacts with the animals. The vet must be genuinely passionate about the job. Without passion, you cannot be assured that he/she will go to all lengths to ensure the best for your cat. He/she must be good with cats. He/she must have complete knowledge on the different practices and techniques that have evolved in veterinary practices. He/she must also make a conscious effort to upgrade his skills and knowledge.

Once you are assured of the behavior of the vet towards you and your cat, you need to get down to the technical and legal aspects.

Is the facility adept in handling emergencies?

How many cages or rooms do they have for the pets that have been admitted there?

Is every staff member educated?

Is the facility licensed?

What are the costs for tests and surgeries?

Is the pricing competitive enough?

What are the insurance policies that they accept?

How many emergencies are handled after regular working hours?

Who takes care of the pets when they are hospitalized?

Are they open to alternative medicines and treatments?

Once you have received satisfactory answers to all the above questions, you can be assured that this facility is best suited for your cat. Remember, the person whom you choose as your vet is going to be your partner in the well being of your beautiful Turkish Angora.

Preparing your Cat for a Vet Visit

Taking a cat to the vet is not easy. If you ask other pet owners, they will tell you that it is definitely not the picnic that you expect it to be. Unknown to most people, cats experience a lot of stress when they are travelling. As a result, it is best that you prepare your cat well for a visit to the vet. Here are five tips that will make the visit less stressful for your cat:

Create a pre-vet routine. Even cats require a good amount of mental preparation before they are taken to the vet. Start by giving your cat a thorough check up from head to toe. This can only be an imitation of the actual test that will take place in the vet's clinic. The idea is to get the cat used to being handled by the vet.

Getting your cat used to the carrier is another way to making the visit less stressful. If your cat learns to associate the carrier with vet visits, it might resist the visit. On the other hand, if you create associations like playtime or even outdoor visits with the carrier, your cat might look forward to the positive activities and be less stressed. You can designate the carrier as a nap place. Throw in its favorite toys and treats inside the carrier to attract your cat towards it.

Of course, the actual journey to the vet is going to create a great deal of stress in the cat. You can reduce this by being affectionate during the drive. Play with it and pet it on the way to keep anxiety levels down.

Make your car cat friendly. Most of the resistance to the visit to the vet is not the clinic itself. It has more to do with the journey to the vet. Usually, cats are taken out in the car only during their visit to the vet. As a result, they automatically associate cars with the negative experiences that they might have had at the vet, including injections and bad tasting medicines. So cats can never stay calm and relaxed inside a car.

However, you can help your cat make positive associations by including drives in the car in your daily routine. You can take the cat for short distances too. Take the car to the park, for instance. Then your cat will stop making negative associations. You can even stop by at the vet's clinic for 5 minutes to get your cat used to the staff there.

The basic idea is to get your cat used to the car. It must learn to be calm and relaxed during these visits. Keeping some toys in the car and allowing it to play during these drives will also help a great deal.

Beat the waiting room blues. One place dreaded by all animals is the waiting room at the clinic. There are several unpleasant sounds like the barking of dogs and even chatter of humans that increase the levels of anxiety in a cat.

Cats are, by nature, solitary animals and do not like being introduced to so many strange sights and sounds at one go. The best thing to do would be to leave your cat in the carrier until it is called in for examination. This gives it a secure hide out and it will be more at ease.

Make sure that the carrier that you are using is large enough. Place a nice cat bed or a cushion inside for it to rest on. You can also leave toys and goodies inside the carrier. A top loading carrier is a must, as it will become impossible for you to get your frightened kitty out of a front loading one.

Special pheromone sprays are available to reduce anxiety and stress in cats during their visit to the vet. These sprays imitate the scent that cats leave when they rub themselves against the legs of their loved ones.

You can also schedule your appointments to the less busy parts of the day. That way, the chaos in the waiting room will be lesser, making your cat feel more relaxed.

Get friendly with your vet. It is good to allow your vet to spend some time with your cat and break the ice. Of course, the vet is going to poke and prod the cat for examination. This becomes less stressful if the cat can look at the vet as a friend rather than a stranger.

Make sure you clear up all queries related to your cat's well being when you visit the vet. Even if it means additional visits, do not shy away from it.

Send items from home for overnight stays. If your cat is due for overnight hospital care, send its favorite items from home. The idea is to keep him/her around familiar scents so that he/she does not get too anxious. There are several routine procedures like neutering that can be extremely stressful for your cat. Making regular visits and sending him/her things from home can really help the cat overcome this anxiety.

You must always work with your vet to ensure the complete well being of your cat. You must trust the knowledge and expertise of your vet if you want him/her to be the best caregiver for your cat.

Usually, vets will be more than willing to lend support in the form of study material to help you understand how you can take care of your cat at home.

Chapter 15. The Cost of Owning a Turkish Angora

Now that you are aware of the basics of cat care, you might begin to wonder how expensive it is to actually take care of one. In comparison to dogs, cats are cheaper to own. However, if you want to put a number on your cat care expenses, here is a clear break up.

1) Initial Costs

Your Cat
$500 (£290) at the least.
A Turkish Angora cat costs about $500 or £290 on average. However, the breed plays a very important role in determining your price range. If your cat comes with a pedigree certificate, it could cost you up to £700. Of course, if you decide to adopt a cat, you will get your cat for free most of the time. Some adoption fees may be charged but they will be less than what you might expect from a breeder.

Vaccinations and de-sexing may be covered in some cases but this is not always going to be the case. Always look to see what a breeder or other place does for this.

Council Registration
$40 (£5)
Every cat needs to be registered under the local council in certain countries. This is necessary to obtain required licenses for your cat.

Desexing
$100-200 (£60 - 120)
This is only if your breeder hasn't taken care of this already. The costs vary from one vet to another. Spaying or neutering is always going to be important to consider.

Microchipping
$50 (£30)

In some countries, microchipping is mandatory. This is a good option to ensure that your cat, if lost, can be reunited with you at the earliest. This works in that a microchip material will be implanted into a safe part of the cat's body. It will be found under the cat's skin. The authorities can use a device to read the data for which the cat is listed to ensure that it will be found and returned to its proper owner over time.

Vaccinations
$50-$70 (£30 - 50)

Never ignore or neglect vaccinations. Refer to the section on vaccinations for more information.

Cat Carriers
$30-$50 (£20 - 30)

You will definitely need a cat carrier to make trips to the vet or travel with your beloved Turkish Angora.

2) Optional Expenses

Scratching Post
$100 approx (£60)

If you want to safeguard your home from havoc, make sure you get your kitty a scratch post. The costs may be higher depending upon the type of post you choose.

Cat Toys
$30 for basics (£20)

There are so many toys available on the market that you can certainly not put a price on this. However, for a basic selection, you will pay about $30. You must not neglect cat toys, as they are necessary for good exercise for your cat.

3) Ongoing Costs

Food
$10 per week (£6)
There are various brands that you get on the market. The price of
the cat food will depend entirely upon what you choose to feed
your cat.

Litter
$8 per week (£5)
This is just an approximation. The costs may vary as per the type
of litter.

Worming Medications
$2.50 per week (£1.5)
These topical medicines need to be re-applied regularly.

Veterinary checks
$70 per year (£60)
This is the cost for routine checkups only. It does not account for
unexpected accidents of illnesses.

Pet Sitter
$10- 25 per day (£6 - 15)
This is an expense that you cannot rule out if you are someone
who travels occasionally or even works late.

Owning a pet is a big responsibility monetarily. It is as good as
having a baby at home. If you think that you might have to
compromise on any of the expenses mentioned above, make sure
you re-think your decision of bringing home a Bombay cat.

4) Insurance

You might also consider taking insurance for your cat. It can
cover many expenses that are associated with taking care of your
care and making sure that it stays as healthy as possible. Usually,

insurance policies are anything between $20 / £12 and $60 / £36 per month. Please be aware that the monthly cost for insurance might increase each year, as your cat gets older.

Conclusion

As we have learned, the Turkish Angora is a beautiful breed of cat, which is loved by a lot of people all over the world. The Turkish Angora, as the name suggests, is a breed from the Turkish city of Ankara. Now it is bred in many parts of the world and pet lovers can easily get the information from where they can get the desired breed of the Turkish Angora cat.

The Turkish Angora cat has long hair, which makes it more suitable for cold environments. Therefore, it is a cat that might not be able to survive in places with hot weather conditions. It is the most preferable cat to be kept as a pet. It is an economical cat and doesn't weigh too much either, which makes it more ideal to be kept at home. The personal characteristics and traits of the cat are admirable.

It comes in different shades of white, brown, yellowish, or a mixture of all. The eyes can either be brown, yellow, blue or black. The blue-eyed Turkish Angora is the most loved cat of all. It is also regarded as one of the most agile cats and it can very swiftly climb a tree or a wall. Therefore, the security and safety of the cat is also of essence.

A cat is a faithful animal and keeps a good bonding with its master. The Turkish Angora cat is just like one of them and there is never any threat of cat losing its way back home. Wherever you take or leave it, no matter how far the place is, the Turkish Angora will surely find its way back home.

The Turkish Angora cat normally has a longer lifespan compared to other breeds of cats. It is also a reason that this cat is preferred by the pet lovers due to the obvious natural affectionate relationship that they develop with their master and vice versa. The affection and bonding between the cat and its masters sometimes get so strong that both couldn't live without each other.

They are also considered a very intelligent cat and can learn a variety of things quickly. They can soon learn how to open the doors, cabinets, and drawers at home.

Although it develops a good bonding with its master, it still doesn't like to be carried in the hands of its master for a long time. After a certain amount of time, the cat starts showing signs of anguish and discomfort, which means that it should be released to the floor and ideally should be fed or play with its toys. Its intelligent nature is also evident when the cat shows that it knows its limitations and space.

Once it is trained, it will never cross the boundary where it shouldn't be going. It quickly gets to know its place.

It is a friendly cat and can easily get settled with other breeds of cats. It can be a challenge for the cat owner who has different pets at home.

Food for the Turkish Angora should essentially be nutrition enriched. Nutrition is important for the cat's body in order to maintain the metabolic process consistent.

Grooming is also important. A well groomed Turkish Angora cat could be a top most candidate of the cat shows. A cat show is the place where most of the pets lovers get to know about different breeds of cats and can also chose to adopt/buy a certain desirable cat as their pet.

The Turkish Angora cat got famous at several cat shows mostly in Europe and some parts of America as well. It got huge appreciation and a lot of people still show great interest, love, and affection to have the Turkish Angora cat as their pet.

Published by IMB Publishing 2014